Mungo
Park

Mark Duffill

NMS Publishing

Published by
NMS Publishing Limited
Royal Museum, Chambers Street, Edinburgh EH1 1JF
© Mark Duffill 1999
Series editor Iseabail Macleod

Other titles available in this series

Miss Cranston
Elsie Inglis
The Gentle Lochiel

Cover: Saddlecloth made of wool, leather and cotton.
Hausa people, Nigeria, 1930s.

**British Library Cataloguing
in Publication Data**
A catalogue record of this book is
available from the British Library

ISBN 1 901663 15 9

Cover design by NMS Publishing Limited
Typeset by Artisan Graphics, Edinburgh
Printed in the United Kingdom by
Cambridge University Press Printing Division

Acknowledgements

I am grateful to the following for advice, assistance and encouragement, including comment and correction of drafts: Susannah Honeyman, Marlene Hinshelwood, Dr Geoffrey Brooker, Professor Brian Harris, formerly of Ahmadu Bello University, Zaria, Nigeria; Dr Henry Nolte and Dr Peter Harris of the Royal Botanic Gardens, Edinburgh. I am also grateful to Mr Arnott Wilson, University Archivist, and the staff of the Special Collections Library within the Library of the University of Edinburgh, for help with the manuscript records relating to Mungo Park; Helen Darling and Rosamund Brown at the Scottish Borders Archive & Local History Centre, Selkirk; Malcolm Beasley and staff at the Botany Library, British Museum (Natural History); Jane Kidd of the Paisley Museum and Art Galleries, Gina Douglas, Librarian, The Linnean Society, London, and more generally staff at the following Libraries, Archives, Museums and Galleries: The British Library, London; The National Archives of Scotland, Edinburgh; National Library of Scotland, Edinburgh; Royal Commission on the Ancient and Historical Monuments of Scotland, Edinburgh; Royal Scottish Academy, Edinburgh; Library of the Royal Botanic Garden, Edinburgh; Sir Walter Scott's Courtroom Museum & Halliwell's House Museum, Selkirk; The Heinz Archive at the National Portrait Gallery, London; Ian Mitchell for Robert Clapperton (Photographer), Selkirk.

I am grateful to the Trustees of the British Library and the British Museum (Natural History) for permission to quote from manuscripts in their collections. I am also grateful to the Scottish Borders Council for permission to quote from manuscripts held at the Scottish Borders Archive and Local History Centre, Library HQ, St Mary's Mill, Selkirk.

My sincere thanks are also due to my patient editor Helen Kemp, and to all the staff of NMS Publishing Limited. Helen Kemp and Iseabail Macleod read and corrected my typescripts, helped me in the development of style, and gave me advice and encouragement throughout.

Illustrations

Cover, 104: National Museums of Scotland. 6, 21: By courtesy of the National Portrait Gallery, London. 25: *Trans Linn Soc* 3 (1797), by permission of the British Library. 38: By permission of the Royal Botanic Garden, Edinburgh. 47: From an engraving in *Travels in Western Africa from the River Gambia to the River Niger* by Major Gray and the late Staff Surgeon Dochard, London, 1825. By permission of the University of Edinburgh Library. 65, 86, 123: From an engraving in *Voyage au Soudan Français...* by J S Gallieni, Paris, 1885. By permission of the British Library. 77: From an engraving in *Voyage dans le Soudan Occidental...* by M E Mage, Paris, 1868. By permission of the University of Edinburgh Library. 84: From a lithograph by G Severeyns in *Sertum Botanicum...* by P-C Van Geel, Brussels, 1836–8. By permission of the Royal Botanic Garden, Edinburgh. 101: By permission of the Paisley Museum and Art Galleries, Renfrewshire Council.

Preface

In this book I have sought to present the story of the life and times of Mungo Park, paying special attention to his background in the Scottish Border country, and to the account he gave of Africa in the book he wrote about his first expedition to that continent, first published exactly two centuries ago. *Travels in the Interior Districts of Africa* is a classic work of travel literature, and I hope that my summary of its contents will give the reader an idea of its author's experiences in West Africa.

My interest in Mungo Park as a subject for biography came in part from the fact that I had lived and worked in West Africa for the best part of a decade, and had the opportunity to travel and to learn something of its vibrant culture and its fascinating and turbulent history. Since leaving Africa, I have also had the pleasure of residing in Scotland for some years and have greatly enjoyed roaming the hills and valleys of that part of Ettrick Forest that Mungo Park knew and loved so well, and learning something of the equally fascinating and tragic history of the Scottish Border country. I hope that both these experiences may have done

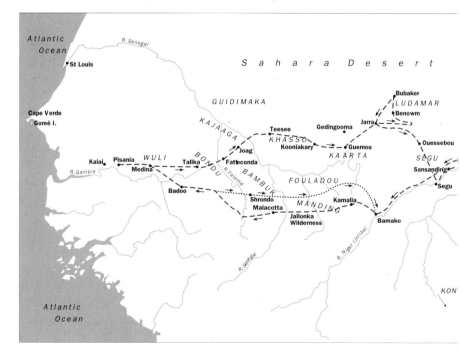

something to sharpen my understanding for the life and times of Mungo Park.

It is appropriate at this point to acknowledge a debt to all previous biographers of Mungo Park, especially James Wishaw, H B, Lewis Grassic Gibbon and Kenneth Lupton. The important 1979 study by the last named, broke much new ground, particularly regarding the background to Mungo Park's second expedition, and in the careful analysis of the reports relating to the events at Bussa and the death of Mungo Park and his companions. My own researches have yielded new material relating to Mungo Park as a medical student at the University of Edinburgh. I also succeeded in locating a short poem by Mungo Park, set to music and published around 1803, and I have pleasure in reproducing the text in Chapter 10.

I have generally retained the original spellings of place and personal names from both the *Travels* and the *Journal*, though in some cases the modern usage has also been given in parentheses. Some of the towns and villages mentioned by Mungo Park no longer exist, while others that do survive will not be found in the atlases and maps available to the general reader.

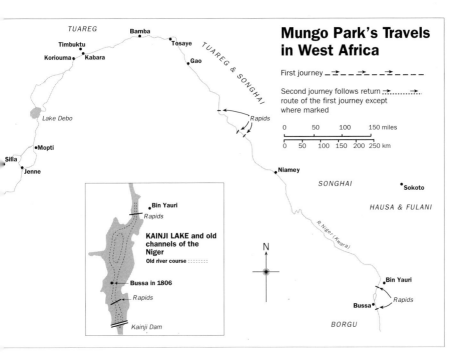

Mungo Park. Watercolour portrait by Thomas Rowlandson, 1805.

1

The Scottish background & Mungo Park's education

Mungo Park was born in the parish of Selkirk, in the Scottish Border country, very probably on 11 September 1771. This is the date recorded in the baptismal register, though in several biographies and other works of reference 10 September is the given date. Mungo bore the same name as his father, who was a tenant farmer at Foulshiels in the valley of the Yarrow Water, about four miles from the ancient burgh of Selkirk. In 1761, Mungo Park the elder, then forty-seven years old, had married the nineteen-year-old Elspeth Hislop, the daughter of a tenant farmer from the same valley. Mungo Park the younger was the seventh of thirteen children, of whom only eight survived into adult life. These were Margaret, Archibald, Jean, Mungo, Alexander, John, Adam and Isobel.

Rolling hills are the dominant feature of the topography of Selkirkshire. These hills and the valleys of the rivers that intersect them — the Tweed, the Yarrow, the Ettrick and many smaller streams — had once been covered by the wild woodland of Ettrick Forest. In this Royal Forest in medieval times, the Kings of Scots came to hunt wild boar, red deer, roe deer, wild white cattle bulls, and other game. Steady encroachment upon the forest for the pasturing of sheep and cattle, and for timber, meant that by the mid-sixteenth century there was little game left, and the forest was well on the way to becoming what it was in Mungo Park's day, a sheep walk, as it largely remains. Within the ancient Royal Forest, there had been many shielings (pasturelands, and roughly constructed shelters on those lands) where serfs looked after livestock, principally sheep, for the Cistercian monks of Melrose Abbey. In the twelfth century, the monks had received from King David I a grant of rights to pasture, wood and pannage (pasturing of swine, or other animals, on woodland products — acorns, beech-mast, etc) in the Royal Forest, rights confirmed and extended by later Kings of Scots. The steading (farmhouse and outbuildings) at Foulshiels may well have had its origins as such a shieling but with the feuing (leasing in perpetuity) of Crown and Church lands from the early sixteenth century, the ownership of Foulshiels and many other steadings in Ettrick Forest passed into the hands of the Scotts of Buccleuch. The tenancy of the farm at Foulshiels was not heritable but at the time Mungo Park was born the tenancy had been in the Park family for two generations, and would pass into the hands of a third when his father died in 1793. Foulshiels was a medium-sized farm for the area, with some arable land in the valley, and pasture for sheep and cattle on the hills. From a rent roll for the Buccleuch estate in the year 1766, we learn that Mungo Park the elder, the tenant at Foulshiels, paid an annual rent of seventy-four pounds to the Duke of Buccleuch, maintained 720 sheep and ten cattle in pasture, and also sowed twenty-six bolls (156 bushels) of grain, the greater part of that probably being oats, with some barley.

The Park family, the guidman (master of the house) and guidwife (mistress of the house), their children, and several farm servants, lived what was essentially a peasant lifestyle in a traditional 'but and ben' house. Typically, these were from thirty to forty-five feet long and from twelve to thirteen feet wide, with low, rough clay, or rough stone walls, with a few windows, and thatched with straw and turfs. Usually, these houses were internally divided into two or three rooms. The 'but' served as kitchen and living room for the whole household, including farm-servants. In the 'but', or in a small room partitioned from it, would be found the box-beds, where the adult daughters of the house and any maidservants would have slept. The other main room, the 'ben' was the private room of the guideman and his wife, though their younger children would also sleep there. It also served as a reception room, where those regarded as social equals or superiors, could be entertained. In the 'ben' the walls would have been plastered and a wooden floor laid down. The 'ben' would have been as well plenished as the guidman and his wife could afford, with a better quality of furniture than that in the 'but', good box-beds: probably one or two chests, perhaps a desk and a clock. The family Bible, and such other books as the family possessed, would have been kept in the 'ben'. Typically, these books would have included works of religion and of Scottish history. If there was an attic above the 'ben', as was often the case, the adult sons of the house and male farm-servants would sleep there, or in its absence would join the horses in the stables.

In such a household food was simple but generally plentiful, the famine years of the 1690s now a distant memory, though there were still occasional years of serious dearth. There were several years in the second half of the eighteenth century when the oat crop failed, as in the year of Mungo Park's birth, and again in 1782, 1795, 1799 and 1800. There was no famine in these years, though people might go hungry, because there was now a second staple — the potato, grown by every farmer and labourer. Virtually all the food consumed in the Park household would have come from the farm itself. Oats were the traditional staple, in the form of porridge and bannocks. Usually, meat was served twice a week at the midday meal, mutton in summer, salt beef in winter. For guests, or on special occasions, lamb, chicken, or fish from the river might be served. Potatoes, dairy products, eggs, kail, pease-meal, barley and possibly honey, all from the farm, would have rounded out the diet.

Much of the clothing for the family would have come from the farm. Wool would have been spun by maidservants, or by the daughters of the house, then woven, fulled and dyed by local craftsmen, before being made up by a tailor from Selkirk. Boots and shoes, from the hide of the beast killed for the winter's supply of salt beef, would also be made up locally, Selkirk being famous for its souters (shoemakers).

The town of Selkirk, standing on a hill overlooking the Ettrick Water, some two miles below its junction with the Yarrow Water, was a Royal Burgh with charters from the Scottish Crown dating back to the fourteenth century. In the late eighteenth century the town was small, with a population of the order of 1,000, mainly engaged in trade and craft occupations, with small-scale farming and pasturing of stock in the extensive common lands. Selkirk was the market town for the county and was controlled by a Town Council representing the Merchants and the Craft Guilds. The town was fortunate in having a grammar school that acquired an excellent reputation during the seventeenth and eighteenth centuries. There was relatively little manufacturing industry in the town, in the late eighteenth century, though in other Border towns, such as Hawick, and in the village of Galashiels, the woollen industry was well established and was about to enter a period of rapid expansion.

We do not know for sure whether Mungo Park the elder was an 'improving tenant', one prepared to experiment with newly introduced farming methods. However, in one biography of his son, the father is described as having been an 'assiduous and successful' farmer, a phrase that suggests intelligent application to his business. There is also evidence to suggest that his landlord, the Duke of Buccleuch, the largest landowner in the county, did give encouragement to 'improving tenants', while retaining the practice of granting tenancies on a yearly basis, a policy generally considered inimical to improvement. Certainly, such evidence as there is does suggest that the elder Mungo Park was a successful farmer, and in late eighteenth-century Lowland Scotland, this would have meant a farmer prepared to try new methods, once their value had been demonstrated. His success as a farmer can be measured to some extent by the fact that he was able to give three of his sons — Mungo, Alexander and Adam — an education that allowed them to enter the professions. Furthermore, when Archibald, his eldest son, obtained the tenancy of another farm, his father supplied the necessary capital. At his death, Mungo Park the elder left significant legacies to his eight surviving children, and an annuity to his widow.

Agricultural improvement was gathering momentum in Lowland Scotland in the second half of the eighteenth century, examples of good farming practice were being set, and knowledge of successful techniques diffused. We can identify some of the innovations that an 'improving tenant' might have made. Without much doubt, the elder Mungo Park's farming interests would have been centred upon sheep. He would have looked for improvements to the local breed, so as to secure better yields in wool and carcass weight. He would also have been interested in finding ways to prevent, control, or cure the diseases that afflicted sheep in the area. From the late 1760s the white-faced sheep, a breed of Cheviot stock crossbred with the black faced sheep, a hardy local breed, was replacing the latter as the breed of choice over much of Selkirkshire. Several herds of the pure Cheviot breed, or of Cheviot stock crossbred with English breeds, such as the Bakewell and the Cowley, were raised in the county during the later eighteenth century, with very satisfactory results in terms of appearance and carcass weight. On the arable side, once enclosure and consolidation of the rigs (the division of land into strips) had taken place, significant improvements to soil fertility could be made through shell marling or liming, manuring, draining and ground levelling, followed by the adoption of appropriate crop rotations. Such rotations might include crops that were relatively new to the south of Scotland, especially turnips and clover. Turnips were being cultivated in Selkirkshire in the 1770s, and by the 1790s there were few tenant farmers in the county who did not grow them. There is a high probability that the elder Mungo Park's success as a farmer would have been based on improvements such as those outlined here.

Mungo Park the elder certainly shared the Scottish belief in the value of a good education, taking the significant step for a man of limited means of hiring a private tutor for a period of several years. The tutor lived in and took responsibility for the children's elementary education, under their father's supervision and direction. This early education would have included Bible study, for Mungo Park the elder would appear to have been a religious man, in the radical tradition of Scottish Presbyterianism, and a member of Selkirk's Secession Church. After some years of private tutoring, Mungo Park the younger was enrolled at Selkirk Grammar School, where he studied English, Latin, mathematics, religious knowledge and perhaps some geography and history. He gained a reputation as a serious and successful scholar, rather quiet and reserved in his manner, and of a somewhat solitary disposition, often going off for long rambles on his own. He was not one of those who made friends easily but those friends he did have were close.

There was also an informal side to young Mungo Park's education. In the family home, he would have heard the legends and ballads of the Borders from farm-servants and neighbours, and from those packmen, journeymen and 'idle sorners' (beggars) who trudged the roads and trackways of Lowland Scotland in the eighteenth century. He developed a lasting interest in and affection for the ballads and stories of his homeland. They reflected the turbulent history of the Borders, many of them dealing with bloody events in local feuds, or with incidents in the wars with England. Among the ballads that derived from local feuds, there are four tragic laments that refer to incidents thought to have taken place in or near the valley of the Yarrow, and considered by many to be among the finest and most moving of all the Border ballads — *Willie's Rare and Willie's Fair, The Douglas Tragedy, The Dowie Houms of Yarrow* and *The Lament of the Border Widow.* There are other ballads in epic or heroic modes that refer to the wars with England or to cross-Border reiving (raiding, robbing, plundering). Among the most notable of these are *Auld Maitland, The Battle of Otterbourne, Chevy Chase, Raid of the Reidswire, The Fray of Suport, Jamie Telfer of the Fair Dodhead,* and *Kinmont Willie.* These ballads, and many others, Mungo Park would have heard, and some of them he is known to have committed to memory. From similar sources he would have heard something of the folk history of the Borders, from William Wallace in Ettrick Forest in 1296–7 waging guerrilla warfare against the English invaders, to the battle at nearby Philiphaugh in 1645, when an Army of the Covenant under the command of David Leslie surprised and routed a Royalist Army under James Graham, Marquis of Montrose.

There were probably other aspects of Mungo Park's informal education, for in eighteenth- and nineteenth-century Scotland there were many largely self-taught men from relatively humble backgrounds, who made important contributions to literature, and to the sciences. Here it is only necessary to mention Robert Burns, and James Hogg, 'the Ettrick Shepherd' in the field of literature. Perhaps of greater significance for Mungo Park were the botanists and horticulturists, such as James Lee, and James Dickson, both local men who retained links with Selkirkshire after moving to England. James Dickson married Mungo Park's elder sister Margaret in 1786 when Mungo was fifteen years old and it is probable that it was he who first fired Mungo Park's interest in natural history, and encouraged his interest in botany.

Mungo Park the elder was of the opinion that his son Mungo would be well suited to a career as a minister, and that given his studious ways and serious character he would be able to 'wag his pow in the poopit' (shake his head in the pulpit) with the best of them. We do not know why Mungo rejected the idea of a career in the church and insisted on the profession of medicine. However, it should be remembered that in late eighteenth-century Britain, the study of medicine was virtually the only way in which it was possible for a bright young man of limited means to obtain an education in the sciences. Perhaps Mungo Park was drawn towards the idea of a career in science, rather than in medicine, through the influence of people whom he knew especially James Dickson. Through his brother-in-law, the young Mungo Park may have caught a glimpse of a world of high intellectual excitement, in which secular understanding and practical improvement, rather than religious conviction, were the ruling passions and to which Scotsmen such as Joseph Black, William Cullen, Adam Ferguson, David Hume, James Hutton, Adam Smith and many others, had made, or would make, important contributions. Furthermore, news of the travels of James Bruce in Ethiopia and the voyages of Captain James Cook in the Pacific Ocean and the Polar Seas might well have captured the imagination of an introspective young man of intelligence and ambition, and given him a taste for travel and adventure in the cause of science.

In 1785, when Mungo Park was fourteen years old, he was apprenticed to Dr Thomas Anderson in Selkirk, though he continued to take some classes in Latin and mathematics at the Grammar School. Apprenticeship was one route into medicine at this time, though it would be followed by attendance at medical school. A medical apprentice would accompany the doctor on his rounds, which in Selkirkshire could involve frequent rides of forty miles and more over very rough country in all kinds of weather. The apprentice would listen, observe, assist, and — hopefully — learn something of the practice of medicine. Much time would also be spent in the dispensary, making up medicines and learning the properties of the constituent drugs.

Mungo Park left his apprenticeship with Dr Anderson in 1788 for the medical school of the University of Edinburgh, certainly the best centre for both medical and scientific education in Britain, perhaps in Europe, at that time. Students came to the Edinburgh medical school from England, Ireland and many European countries, as well as America, and the East and West Indies. Several of the most distinguished medical educators and practical scientists of the day, notably Joseph Black (chemistry) and Alexander Monro *secundus* (anatomy and surgery), were teaching courses at the Edinburgh medical school that Mungo Park had the opportunity to attend.

Some observations about the practice of medicine and medical education in late eighteenth century Britain are necessary before considering the course of study that Mungo Park followed at the University of Edinburgh. There was no standard method of entry into the profession, this being in part the result of the historic division of medicine between physicians, surgeons and apothecaries; and in part the result of an absence of any national system of registration and regulation of medical practitioners. Indeed there were many medical practitioners with no formal qualifications whatsoever, and in rural areas and among the urban poor, such medical services as were available probably depended as much on men and women skilled in the arts of folk medicine, as it did on formally trained physicians and surgeons.

In Britain, medical education and training was diverse, a reflection of the historic divisions within the profession. Typically, the route followed by those who became physicians was through the academic study of medicine at a university, while surgeons and apothecaries followed apprenticeships. However, by the late eighteenth century, surgical apprenticeships were frequently followed by a course of study at a university, or in Edinburgh at the College of Surgeons. It was also possible to get a medical education through private anatomy schools, and in certain hospitals, especially in London. The diversity of methods of entry into medicine and the different requirements of particular groups of students, meant that it was impossible to regulate the qualifications necessary for medical practice without the introduction of changes to the structure and organisation of the medical profession, and for this to happen legislative action was required. In the *laissez-faire* climate of the times, Parliament was reluctant to intervene.

At the University of Edinburgh, where there were no religious restrictions on entry, where courses were relatively cheap and the lectures were given in English, there was no obligation on students to graduate, and they could choose the courses they required. Some already had experience, or had studied elsewhere, or intended doing so, perhaps at Leiden or Paris, or at the hospitals and private anatomy schools in London.

In the late eighteenth century, only a relatively small proportion of the medical students at the University of Edinburgh considered it necessary to take, or could afford to take, the full range of seven courses that the regulations required for a degree in medicine. These courses were anatomy and surgery, chemistry, botany, *materia medica* and pharmacy, medical theory, medical practice and the clinical lectures. The time taken to complete the full course leading to graduation was generally three years, though some students took longer, while with exemptions others might complete in two years. Exemptions from courses and examinations might be granted where a student could provide evidence of study at another institution, or relevant experience. Students intending to graduate were required to pass the examinations and write a dissertation in Latin, which they would be required to defend in that language. Though clinical studies in Britain were pioneered in Edinburgh, with lectures held in wards at the Royal Infirmary, only a minority of all students registered for them, though they were followed by the majority of graduating students. These clinical lectures do not seem to have been particularly well organised and it was possible for a student to graduate with no more experience of patients than what he might have heard and seen at lectures in crowded wards. Students had little or no opportunity for 'face to face' experience with patients. Those who had served an apprenticeship with surgeons or apothecaries had advantages in this respect, a fact that was resented by the gentlemen medical students, who tended to look down on apprentices and ex-apprentices as 'vulgar tradesmen'.

Those students who did not intend to graduate took only those courses that they considered necessary, or could afford, in order to set up in practice, or secure employment. Opportunities for employment existed with the army, the navy, the East India Company and in some few other fields, including the slave trade after 1788. For employment in the armed services, or with the EIC, a powerful patron was more important than a degree in medicine. With a powerful patron, some medical education and training, a young man stood an excellent chance of obtaining a post as surgeon or assistant surgeon in the armed services and the EIC, though competition for positions with the EIC was particularly keen. Once the patron had exercised his powers on behalf of a client, all that the EIC required from the client was a licence from the Company of Surgeons in London, usually granted after a short oral examination, and payment of a fee.

From the records of the University of Edinburgh it can be shown that Mungo Park took Joseph Black's course in chemistry and Alexander Monro's course in anatomy and surgery. He also took the courses given by Andrew Duncan (medical theory), James Gregory (medical practice) and Daniel Rutherford (botany) between November 1788 and the end of July 1791. Mungo took anatomy and surgery in his first and second years, chemistry in his second and third years, medical theory in his second year, medical practice and botany in his third year. Mungo appears to have had no intention of graduating, though his experience as an apprentice might well have secured him exemption from examination in *materia medica* and clinical studies.

It should be noted that the course in botany at the medical school was only held in the summer months, between the first week in May and the end of July. Letters from Mungo to a friend in Selkirk, now in the National Archives of Scotland, demonstrate that he was resident in Edinburgh in May and June 1791, while the records of the University of Edinburgh, though capable of another interpretation, suggest that he completed the course in botany in 1791.

The formal records of matriculation and registration give us no more than the bare bones of Mungo's life as a student in Edinburgh, but he is mentioned in the records of the Chirurgo-Physical Society, one of the student societies that flourished in the city in the late eighteenth and early nineteenth century. This Society was founded in 1788, and Mungo is recorded as having presented three papers in the period 1789–91. The subjects covered in these manuscript dissertations are jaundice (*Icterus*), ringworm (*Taenia capitis*) and scurvy (*Scorbutus*), the manuscript of the latter being incomplete in the bound volume of the Society's dissertations held in the Library of the University of Edinburgh. All three are diseases that he would probably have seen during his apprenticeship with Dr Anderson.

In his paper on *Taenia capitis*, given on 16 April 1790, Mungo writes with some feeling about a form of treatment known as the Pitched Cap, which he regarded as cruel and dangerous, especially to children. This treatment, as Mungo described it, consisted in coating areas of the head, or even the whole head, with pitch. In due course this Pitched Cap would be peeled off, removing the infected skin and all the hair! He argued that this treatment should only be used when all other methods had failed, and then only by application to small areas of the head. Mungo's strong objection to the Pitched Cap as a method of treatment suggests that he might have experienced it himself, and would have seen it used. From his description of this method of treatment for ringworm, there is no doubting the terrible pain and serious inflammation that would accompany the removal of the Pitched Cap. We may note that earlier in the month of April 1790, Mungo presented a paper on scurvy, typically a disease associated with sailors, but it may be going too far to infer from this that he was already considering employment as a sea going surgeon.

One of Mungo's biographers writing in 1835, who had talked with Mungo's widow and his brother John, among others, observed that Mungo was particularly fond of botany and would follow this 'favourite study with great ardour during the summer months, which his vacations permitted him to spend in the country'. The same biographer also makes an interesting comment on Mungo's attitude to his studies and the profession of medicine, observing that while he:

> never appears to have taken much interest in the healing art he displayed in its acquisition his usual perseverance; and was, if not an enthusiastic, by no means an unsuccessful student...

Several of Mungo Park's biographers have represented him as a quiet and diligent student, but the suggestion that he was a less then enthusiastic student raised doubts in my mind. At a very late stage in the preparation of this book, I learnt that a collection of letters from Mungo Park, written between 1790 and 1794, had been seen in the Peebles Burgh Archives in the 1920s. A search revealed that they are now to be found in the National Archives of Scotland, Edinburgh, whose staff were kind enough to provide me with a summary of their contents.

The letters, all of them written to a William Laidlaw in Selkirk, revealed a rather different Mungo to the reserved and diligent student described by some of his biographers. From the letters we gain an impression of a young man with an active social life, who mixed with the aspiring young *literati* of the city, participated in debates at The Pantheon, a famous Edinburgh debating society, attended the theatre, made fishing expeditions with friends and wrote poetry. His letters make passing reference to a serial publication *The Bee, or Literary Weekly Intelligencer....* A search of this publication brought to light a poem 'On the death of William Cullen, MD' by MP, Braes of Yarrow, 4 June 1791. (Cullen, who had been Professor of Medicine at the University of Edinburgh, died in February, 1790.)

The letters reveal that on at least two occasions Mungo addressed the audience at Pantheon debates in Scots verse, and he may have taken part in a debate on the relative merits of the poetry of Allan Ramsay and Robert Fergusson that took place on 14 April 1791. If he did do so, as has been claimed by one of his biographers, his interest in these two distinctively Scottish poets, and his own use of Scots verse in public debate, may be seen as a conscious affirmation of national identity, as well as a love of Scots poetry. Many of his contemporaries, seeking careers in England and status in polite society, were only too eager to abandon the vernacular, increasingly regarded as the speech of the poor and uncouth.

In Edinburgh, in the late 1780s and early 1890s, Mungo Park's informal education would have been continued. He would have met young men from many different places, and from many different backgrounds, though there is some evidence to suggest that there was little social mixing across the classes, or between students of different nationalities. In the background there was the raw and vibrant city itself, changing rapidly, but in many respects still much the same as the Edinburgh celebrated in the poetry of Allan Ramsay and Robert Fergusson.

The patronage of Sir Joseph Banks, and the voyage to Sumatra.

When Mungo Park completed his medical studies at the University of Edinburgh in the summer of 1791 he faced an uncertain future. He certainly did not have access to the resources that would allow him to set up in practice on his own account, and there is no evidence to suggest that he was invited to join any established medical practice. Dr Anderson, his former master, would not have been in a position to offer him anything more than a temporary position, as his son Alexander, Mungo's best friend, was likely to qualify in 1793, and was probably expected to join his father's practice. It is possible that Mungo helped out Dr Anderson during 1791–2, but there is no evidence either way. However, it would appear that Mungo was often seen in and around Selkirk at that time, and this led his biographer Lewis Grassic Gibbon to suggest that Mungo was 'a stickit doctor', that is to say a doctor without a practice, or employment.

Gibbon also suggested that when Mungo Park and James Dickson made a botanical expedition into the Highlands of Scotland in the summer of 1792, Mungo told his brother-in-law that he had an extreme distaste for the life of a general practitioner in rural Scotland, and sought his help in finding alternative employment. Though we cannot be sure about the date, it is certain that Mungo did seek help from James Dickson, a friend of Sir Joseph Banks, who was perhaps the best placed man in Britain to offer patronage to aspiring and ambitious young men with a scientific education and a desire to travel.

James Dickson played a most important role in the development of Mungo Park's career and some obervations about his own history are necessary at this point. He was born to poor parents at Traquair, some eight miles from Foulshiels on the drove road over the Minchmoor. As a boy he had worked in the gardens at Traquair House, where he gained a knowledge of the arts of horticulture, and developed a keen interest in botany. Moving to London as a young man, he is recorded as having worked at nurseries to the west of the city, including that of Jeffrey & Co. in Kensington, and at a nursery in Hammersmith, very probably the famous Vineyard nursery, owned by his fellow countrymen James Lee and Lewis Kennedy. He may also have worked as a gardener at one or more of the large estates on the outskirts of the city, before setting up his own business as a seedsman and nurseryman in Covent Garden in 1772. During James Dickson's early years in London, perhaps whilst working at the Vineyard nursery, he made the acquaintance of the young Joseph Banks, who as a student at Oxford became passionately interested in botany and frequently visited the Vineyard nursery in search of the exotic plants that were raised there from specimens brought to Britain by travellers and collectors.

James Dickson and Joseph Banks became good friends, with Banks encouraging Dickson to develop his interests in botanical science, allowing him open access to his fine library, and introducing him to others with similar interests. Through use of the library, contact with natural philosophers from Joseph Banks' circle and tireless application, James Dickson made himself an authority in one of the most difficult areas in the science of botany, the cryptogams — ferns, mosses, algae, fungi, etc, with a special interest in the mosses and liverworts. With Sir Joseph Banks, and a few others, James Dickson was instrumental in founding both the Linnean Society in 1788, and the Horticultural Society of London, forerunner of the Royal Horticultural Society, in 1808.

James Dickson is known to have made several botanical expeditions to Scotland between 1785 and 1792, and it is possible that Mungo Park accompanied him on more than one of them. James Dickson gave a paper on the plants he had found in 1789 and 1792 to a meeting of the Linnean Society on 5 February 1793, subsequently published in the Society's *Transactions*. There is evidence that while James Dickson was a first-class field botanist, described as 'lynx-eyed' by a fellow naturalist, he had problems writing up his researches in Latin, and is known to have turned

Sir Joseph Banks. Portrait in oils by Thomas Phillips, 1810. By courtesy of the National Portrait Gallery.

to others for assistance. Perhaps James Dickson received some help from Mungo Park, who probably had a sufficient command of scientific Latin, having just completed the botany course at Edinburgh. Whatever the truth of the matter, it is a fact that James Dickson, one of the 'Founding Fellows' of the Linnean Society, successfully proposed Mungo Park for Associate Membership of the Society on 20 November 1792. Was this James Dickson's way of acknowledging Mungo's assistance during their botanical expeditions in Scotland, and perhaps also in the work of preparing a paper for presentation?

It is not known when Mungo Park was first introduced to Sir Joseph Banks, a meeting that must have been arranged by James Dickson. Gibbon has suggested that at their first meeting Mungo was so tongue-tied and

21

awkward that Sir Joseph could make nothing of him and declined to help him. This seems unlikely in view of what Mungo's letters to William Laidlaw reveal about his participation in public debates whilst a student at the University of Edinburgh, but it possible he could have been somewhat overawed in the presence of the President of the Royal Society. What seems more likely is that Sir Joseph had nothing immediately available in the way of patronage, and he might have wanted evidence of serious scientific application from the young man who sought his help. Mungo's participation in the expedition to the Highlands of Scotland in 1792 may even have been suggested to James Dickson by Sir Joseph Banks as furnishing an opportunity to test Mungo's application and seriousness of purpose.

Mungo Park was in London in late October 1792, following the completion of the summer expedition to the Highlands of Scotland, and it was probably around this time that Sir Joseph Banks took the decision to exercise his powers of patronage in Mungo's favour. Sir Joseph had connections with the East India Company, and he made use of these to secure Mungo the post of Assistant Surgeon on one of the Company's ships. However, before Mungo could take up this position, he was required to demonstrate his competence for the assigment through an oral examination at Surgeon's Hall in London, and this he successfully did in January 1793.

Mungo Park was assigned to the *Worcester*, outward bound for Benkulen on the south-west coast of the island of Sumatra, where the East India Company had several trading stations, from which the principal export was pepper. Benkulen was generally thought of as a fever-ridden hell-hole, and a posting to Sumatra was looked upon by most EIC servants as something close to a death sentence. At Benkulen there was none of the social life to be found at Calcutta, Madras or Bombay, and the opportunities for profitable private trading were limited.

The assignment of Mungo Park to a ship bound for Sumatra was probably accidental, but it is possible that it could have been at Sir Joseph Banks' request. One of Sir Joseph's friends with an East India Company background was William Marsden, who had served at Fort Marlborough, the Company's trading station at Benkulen, from 1771–9. On Marsden's return to Britain, he had been invited by Sir Joseph Banks to join the informal circle of savants, who often met for 'philosophical breakfasts' at

Sir Joseph's house in Soho Square. Encouraged by Sir Joseph Banks and others, Marsden wrote a *History of Sumatra*, first published in London in 1783. Marsden's book, which was well received, covered the island's political history and its physical geography, natural history and ethnography. Marsden acknowledged that he had paid relatively little attention to the zoology of the coast of Sumatra, and it is possible that Sir Joseph Banks, or Marsden, may have suggested to Mungo Park that the ichthyology of the Sumatran coast would repay further study. Both Sir Joseph Banks and James Dickson would have advised Mungo on the collection of botanical specimens, and on their care during the long voyage home.

Commander John Hall was the captain of the *Worcester* with a crew of 105 officers and men. Mungo Park would have joined the ship at Gravesend, some days before sailing, to meet Richard Lane, the chief surgeon, and to be introduced to Commander Hall and other officers. The *Worcester's* cargo consisted mainly of stores for Fort Marlborough and the other trading stations on the Sumatra coast. However, since the trade for pepper and some few other commodities in Sumatra was almost entirely dependent on cash payments in silver, outward-bound Indiamen often carried large amounts of treasure. The *Worcester* was no exception, and twelve chests and one half chest of silver bullion were taken on board the ship some days before she sailed from Gravesend on 18 February 1793.

Britain and France were now at war, so Indiamen with their valuable cargoes sailed in convoy with a naval escort whenever possible. Off Portsmouth, the *Worcester* received seven passengers bound for Benkulen, and sailed in convoy with seven other Indiamen and two Royal Navy escorts on 5 April. The voyage to Benkulen took almost twenty weeks and was uneventful, apart from some bad weather in the Atlantic, and in the Southern Ocean, to the south of the Cape of Good Hope and the Mascarene Islands. Both naval escorts and one Indiaman left the convoy while it was still in the Atlantic. The *Worcester* together with the *Minerva*, an Indiaman bound for China via the Sunda Straits, separated from the remaining Bengal-bound Indiamen, in the Indian Ocean and made their landfall of Christmas Island, south of Java, on 9 August. Two days later the *Minerva* entered the Sunda Straits, and on 21 August the *Worcester* anchored off Benkulen, moving to a secure mooring on Rat Island the following day. After the passengers and treasure had been disembarked, the unloading of the cargo would have commenced, the labour probably undertaken by the African and Malagasay slaves the East India Company imported from Madagascar.

The loading of the *Worcester's* return cargo for the East India Company commenced on 16 September. It consisted of just under 600 tons of black pepper and some twenty tons of white pepper, destined for the London market; and thirty-nine large casks of arrack and one large cask of sugar, consigned to St Helena, where the ship would call on the return voyage. The *Worcester* also received cargo from the private trade of Commander Hall and other officers, and the ship's log refers to over 100 chests of benjamin (benzoin, a fragrant resin from the tree *Styrax benzoin*, native to Sumatra and Java, used as incense, and in medicine), a quantity of cassia (*Cinnamomum cassia*, a substitute for the true cinnamon of Ceylon — *Cinnamomum zeylanica*), and several large casks of arrack, probably intended for the London market.

All the ship's officers, including Mungo Park, enjoyed the privilege of private trade. If Mungo had had the resources, he could have shipped home two tons of goods (nothing in comparison with the Commander's privilege of thirty-eight tons on the homeward voyage). It is probable that Mungo did engage in private trade while at Benkulen, as he appears to have repaid a loan of fifty pounds shortly after his return to Britain, and he could not have done this from his salary. We do not know what Mungo traded for, probably with cash in the form of silver, but as a surgeon he would have had some knowledge of the valuable oriental drugs sought by apothecaries and physicians in Britain, and he may well have sought out the Javanese and Chinese traders who stocked such commodities.

During the three months the *Worcester* was at Benkulen Mungo would have had plenty of time to collect botanical specimens for Sir Joseph Banks, and to undertake a study of fish from the waters round Benkulen. He made drawings and watercolour sketches of some twenty different fish species and recorded in detail their measurements and appearance. The drawings and watercolours are now in the Zoology Library of the British Museum (Natural History), and some botanical specimens that he collected in Sumatra are in the same museum's herbarium collection.

The *Worcester* sailed from Benkulen on 14 November, with ten passengers. Eight days out the ship was struck by a cyclone, losing some sails and suffering other damage. The voyage across the Indian Ocean

Perca lunulata. *Fish from Sumatra, new to science, recorded by Mungo Park, 1793.*

was otherwise uneventful and the *Worcester* came to the anchorage at St Helena on 20 January 1794. The Company's arrack and sugar were unloaded, and the passengers put ashore to await the arrival of the homeward-bound Bengal convoy. Four Indiamen arrived on 11 February, and joined by the *Worcester*, two whalers and one sealer, left for England on 18 February. At St Helena the *Worcester* received six more passengers, five of them described as 'Invalids' in the ship's log.

The Indiamen exercised their guns on a fairly regular basis after leaving St Helena but had no occasion to use them in earnest and the convoy came to anchor in St Helen's Roads, off the Isle of Wight, on 23 April. The *Worcester* was immediately boarded by officers of the Royal Navy Impress Service and some forty of her seamen were 'pressed'. After the passengers were disembarked, the convoy continued on up the Channel reaching Gravesend on 2 May.

From the log of the *Worcester*, and other sources relating to the work of sea going surgeons in the late eighteenth century, it is possible to gain some idea of the work that would have been done by Richard Lane and Mungo Park. They had three seriously ill patients to look after at various times, not to mention the 'Invalids' who joined the ship at Saint Helena. On the outward voyage, a member of the crew suffered a serious fall and three weeks later died from his injuries. At Benkulen another member of the crew died, most probably from fever. Homeward bound, one passenger,

25

already a sick man when he joined the ship at Benkulen, died on the last leg of the voyage. Broken bones, cuts and bruises sustained by officers and men in the working of the ship would have needed attention, and in all probability there would have been more than one case of fever while the ship was at Benkulen. No doubt there would also have been cases of venereal disease, dysentery and other gastro-intestinal disorders to attend to, and perhaps a tooth or two to be pulled. The surgeons would have had to keep an eye open for scurvy, and for the dreaded diseases of typhus and plague, carried by fleas from the rats invariably present on board ships.

On his arrival in London, early in May 1794, Mungo received from Margaret Dickson the not unexpected news of their father's death, almost one year previously. Before leaving for Scotland Mungo called on Sir Joseph Banks to pay his respects and to deliver to his patron a number of botanical specimens, and the drawings and watercolours of the fish he had studied in Sumatra. At their meeting, Mungo Park offered his services for any project involving travel in the interests of science that Sir Joseph might have in mind. If nothing else offered, then Mungo appears to have been ready to return to the East Indies as a ship's assistant surgeon. However, Sir Joseph Banks did have something in mind for the enthusiastic young man — a journey to Timbuktu and beyond! Banks promised to put Mungo's name before the General Meeting of the African Association, due to take place before the end of the month. Though no firm offer was made at this stage, the backing of Sir Joseph Banks was crucial, and Mungo Park left London for Scotland with high expectations of being appointed by the African Association to undertake an exploring mission to the interior of Africa.

3

The geography of West Africa & the African Association

In the 1780s, European geographers and cartographers had a reasonably complete knowledge of the basic geography of the planet, with the exception of three important areas — the two Poles, and the interior of the African continent. Captain Cook and other voyagers had largely unlocked the secrets of the Pacific and Southern Oceans; Asia and the Americas were well enough known in general terms, though much detailed surveying and mapping of very large areas remained to be done. Such knowledge as Europeans had of the interior of Africa was derived from classical antiquity, supplemented by material from a very few Arab travellers and geographers and a few relatively recent sources.

The interior of West Africa was almost as poorly known as the interior of the rest of the continent, and it was only in the extreme west — Senegambia — that Europeans had penetrated more than a few miles inland from the coast. In that region, using the two navigable rivers — Senegal and Gambia — the Portuguese, followed and then ousted by the English and the French, had penetrated a few hundred miles into the interior, driven by a search for the gold of Bambuk. From this region, and several others, gold had long been traded with Arab, Berber and Jewish merchants from North Africa who crossed the Sahara Desert, along well-established routes. These North African traders also traded for slaves, ivory, pepper and some few other commodities. The Portuguese, who explored along the Senegambia coast and on the Senegal and Gambia rivers, from the fifteenth century, were quick to seize opportunities for trade in the area. Like the North African merchants, they were principally interested in gold, slaves, ivory and pepper. Slaves were shipped to the Canaries and Madeira to labour in the sugar plantations established in those islands, and also to Portugal itself, mainly for domestic service. With the European colonisation of the Americas, and the subsequent development of gold- and silver-mining in Spanish America, the creation of systems of plantation agriculture in Brazil, the Caribbean islands, and the southern colonies of British North America, the need of the European colonists for labour created an insatiable demand for African slaves. From the Senegambia region alone, modern estimates suggest that around 337,000 slaves were shipped to the Americas, the Atlantic Islands and Europe between 1700 and 1809. The English slave-traders are estimated to have taken just over two thirds of that number, the French just under a quarter, the balance having been carried by the Portuguese, Americans, Dutch, Danes, and others. In total the Senegambia is thought to have supplied only one twentieth of the total number of slaves shipped from West and West-Central Africa (Senegambia to Southern Angola) during that period.

The Portuguese, having sent missions to Mali in 1534 and to Timbuktu in 1565, certainly knew a good deal about the West African interior, but for the most part they kept their knowledge to themselves. A few English and French traders and travellers in the Senegambia region did publish accounts of their travels and while their books contained much useful information about that region and its peoples, derived from personal observation, these authors found it extremely difficult to obtain reliable information relating to the far interior. What they were told was often contradictory and confusing, particularly when attempts were made to relate such information to received ideas of the geography of Africa.

There were two main problems: the first had to do with the great river that all reports suggested flowed through West Africa. Where did it rise, in what direction did it flow, and where did it end? The second problem was related to the first, in that it was widely believed that a great range of mountains, sometimes referred to as the Mountains of the Moon, ran unbroken across Africa, to the south of this great river, along a line that roughly followed latitude 10°N. It was assumed that these mountains acted as a barrier, preventing the great river from finding an outlet to the Atlantic Ocean to the south of that latitude.

The existence of a great river in West Africa that flowed from the west towards the east was known to the Greek historian and geographer Herodotus, writing in the fifth century BC. He recorded, though he did not endorse, the contemporary opinion that this river eventually joined the Nile of Egypt. The Romans also knew of a great eastward-flowing river in West Africa and named it 'Nigir', from which is derived the name by which the river is known today. The Græco-Egyptian geographer Ptolemy, writing in the second century AD, also held the opinion that the Niger flowed from the west towards the east, and terminated in a lake. He correctly located its source in mountainous country close to the sources of the westward-flowing rivers known to us as the Senegal and Gambia, but in no way linked to them.

There were only two important texts from Arab sources dealing with the geography of the interior of Africa that were available to the European geographers of the eighteenth century. The first was that of Abu 'Abd Allah Muhammad ibn Muhammad al-Sharif al-Idrisi, known to the European geographers as the Xeriff Edrisi; the second that of Al-Hasan ibn Muhammad al-Wazzan al-Zayyati, also known as Yuhanna al-Asad, and better known in Europe as Leo Africanus.

The Sharif al-Idrisi wrote a book of geography, usually known in Europe as Roger's Book (*Kitab Roger*) for the Christian ruler of Sicily, King Roger II, completing it in AD 1154. An abridged version was printed in Rome in 1592. Al-Idrisi was in the possession of much information from travellers who had crossed the Sahara and visited *Bilad as-Sudan* (The Land of the Blacks). He attempted to integrate this information with Ptolemy's account of the Nile of Egypt (*Nil Misr*), with most unfortunate results. Al-Idrisi accepted Ptolemy's argument for the existence of a lake in the far interior of Africa from which flowed the Nile of Egypt. He then added to that argument by asserting that the Nile of the Sudan (*Nil as-Sudan*) also flowed out of that lake to the far west of Africa, directly to the south of the Sahara Desert. What al-Idrisi had done was reverse the direction of flow of the Niger from that proposed by the classical authors, thereby creating great problems for the European geographers and cartographers, who took him to be a truly authoritative source.

The manuscript of *The Description of Africa* by Leo Africanus was written in Italian, in Italy, in the 1520s. It was printed in 1550, and shortly after that was translated into both Latin and French. Al-Hasan ibn Muhammad al-Wazzan al-Zayyati, or Leo Africanus, was a Moroccan diplomat, who was captured by Sicilian pirates in 1519 and offered to Pope Leo X, of the Medici family of Florence. The Pope took him into his service and had him baptised as a Christian. Leo wrote *The Description of Africa* at the request of another Pope, Clement VII (Giulio de Medici), completing it in 1526. (Clement VII had personal as well as scholarly and political reasons for an interest in Africa. In the year 1510, Giulio de Medici, at the age of seventeen and already a Cardinal, is believed to have fathered a son by Simonetta, a black serving woman in the Medici household. Simonetta's son Alessandro was acknowledged as a Medici and in 1532, at the behest of the Pope and the Emperor Charles V, he was appointed hereditary Duke of Florence. He was assassinated in 1537 by a distant cousin, Lorenzaccio de Medici.)

As a Moroccan diplomat Leo had travelled to the interior of West Africa on two occasions, and had visited many important places, including Djenne, Timbuktu, Gao, Katsina, Kano, Borno and Kanem. The observations of Leo Africanus regarding the course and direction of flow of the Niger contain several ambiguities, but he was understood by the European geographers to have confirmed the opinion, derived from al-Idrisi, that it flowed from east to west. He certainly rejected the idea that it flowed from the west to empty itself into a large lake in the interior. Leo Africanus knew the text of a geographical work by a minor aristocrat of Muslim Spain, Abu 'Ubayd 'Abd Allah ibn 'Abd al-'Aziz al-Bekri (died AD 1094), who was particularly well informed about *Bilad as-Sudan*, but whose work was unknown in Europe until the 1820s. Al-Bekri clearly indicated the area in which the Niger rises, noted its north-easterly flow towards Timbuktu, and change of direction to the south-east after passing that city. Unfortunately, al-Bekri used the same name — *Nil* — to refer to both the Niger and the Senegal, as well as to the Nile of Egypt, though a careful reading of the text demonstrates that he was referring to different rivers in his account of West Africa. Leo Africanus never visited the far west (Senegambia), so had no opportunity to relate al-Bekri's account of that region to his own observations. The ambiguities relating to the Niger in Leo's work probably reflect some confusion, some lapses in memory and almost certainly some pressure to conform to received ideas of the geography of West Africa. While European geographers thought that al-

Idrisi and Leo Africanus were in agreement as to an east to west flow of the Niger, they recognised that in some respects the accounts of the West African interior given by the two Arab authors were difficult to reconcile with one another.

European knowledge of the geography of the interior of West Africa, right down to the 1720s, may be roughly summarised. The existence of the Niger, or *Nil as-Sudan*, issuing from a lake deep in the interior, flowing from east to west, probably dividing into two or more arms some considerable distance from the Atlantic, and flowing into that ocean as the Senegal and Gambia, or some third river, was assumed to be a fact. The location of a number of states and important cities, most of them situated on or near the *Nil as-Sudan*, was thought to be roughly known. Finally, the existence of a great range of mountains, running from the interior of Sierra Leone to the other side of the African continent, was also assumed to be a fact, largely on the basis of what al-Idrisi had written. Leo Africanus had written of mountains to the south of Kano and the extreme cold of winter in that area. He also referred to mountains in parts of Borno, and was told that there were mountains to the south-west of the country of Melli, which lay far to the south-west of Timbuktu. There was sufficient in Leo's text to confirm the European geographers in the belief that a great mountain range did run across the African continent.

In the early eighteenth century, the French geographer and cartographer G de L'Isle published maps that made use of information collected in the Senegambia region by André Brue, the Commandant General of the Senegal Company. These maps overturned the prevailing European interpretation of the geography of West Africa, by separating the Senegal and Gambia rivers from the Niger and placing the source of all three rivers in mountainous country to the south-west of Timbuktu. Furthermore, de L'Isle turned the direction of flow of the Niger through 180 degrees, to show the river flowing from the west towards the east, and terminating in a lake situated in Borno. In 1749, another French geographer, J B d'Anville, who accepted most of de L'Isle's amendments, rejected the idea that the Niger ended in a land locked lake in Borno, and published a map that acknowledged his ignorance of the river's termination, leaving the matter open. D'Anville's map, with its blank spaces and unanswered questions, obliged geographers and cartographers to face the fact that the information they had about the Niger and the lands through which it flowed was either non-existent, or confused and unreliable.

Between the publication of d'Anville's map in 1749 and the late 1780s, no significant advances in European knowledge of the geography of the West African interior were recorded. Indeed, Major James Rennell, the leading English geographer of the day, continued to maintain that the Niger flowed from east to west. He accepted that the Niger did not join the Senegal and Gambia rivers, but was unable to say what course it followed after passing Timbuktu.

In the late 1780s no European had knowingly seen the Niger, and next to nothing was known for certain about the river and the lands through which it flowed. The questions the geographers were asking were these. Did the Niger flow from the east or from the west? If the Niger flowed from the west did it join the Nile of Egypt? If the Niger did not join the Nile of Egypt, then did it flow into a great lake, or morass, in the interior? If it did none of these things, then what did it do?

In 1788 a group of twelve gentlemen - six Scotsmen, four Englishmen and two Irishmen -, all members of a dining club that met regularly at a tavern in London's West End, resolved to create an organisation, to be called The African Association, whose principal objective would be the collection of information relating to the geography of the interior of Africa. Six members of the dining club were Fellows of the Royal Society, among them Sir Joseph Banks, who largely directed the work of the African Association during the period in which it sponsored active exploration. Initially the founders of the African Association seem to have been primarily motivated by a desire to increase knowledge of the geography of the African interior, though it may be noted that all of them appear to have been broadly supportive of the movement for the abolition of the slave trade. However, as they were all well aware, knowledge could create commercial opportunities and Africa was already a significant market for the products of British industry, though most of that commerce was directly related to the slave trade.

The members of the dining club, having resolved to form the African Association, quickly adopted a constitution and chose Sir Joseph Banks and Henry Beaufoy to be Treasurer and Secretary, assisted by a committee of three. An annual subscription of five guineas was fixed and applications for membership were invited. Within days of the founding of the

Association two men were recruited to travel from North Africa into the interior, with the object of penetrating as far as they could toward the great river, and to gather useful information. The first to leave was John Ledyard, an American adventurer, who was known to Sir Joseph Banks. Ledyard was in London following a journey through Russia and Siberia, and when Sir Joseph asked him if he would be interested in an African expedition, he enthusiastically accepted the idea. The plan was for Ledyard to travel to Cairo and proceed south into Nubia, from whence it was hoped he might be able to make his way to West Africa. Ledyard reached Cairo and sent back some useful information about caravan routes to the south and west. Unfortunately, Ledyard died in Cairo, having accidentally poisoned himself.

Ledyard was followed by Simon Lucas, who as a youth had been a slave in Morocco. He was fluent in Arabic and in 1788 he held the official position of Oriental Interpreter to the Court of St James. The Committee of the African Association appointed Lucas to travel to Tripoli in Libya, from where it was hoped he might be able to join a caravan proceeding south across the Sahara. Lucas obtained leave of absence, and left London in August 1788. He was well received in Tripoli, and joined a caravan, but did not get far. At Mesurata some 120 miles east of Tripoli, learning of serious disturbances in the Fezzan, he decided to turn back. However, Lucas did return with useful information about the Fezzan, and the trade routes across the Sahara to Katsina and Borno.

More useful information on trade routes was obtained from British consuls in Morocco and in Tunis. Still more information was gathered from two Moroccan visitors to Britain, Ben Ali in 1788 and Shabeni in 1790. Ben Ali's information, and some part of that from Shabeni, confirmed the intelligence gathered by Ledyard, Lucas and the consuls. However, a large part of the information supplied by Shabeni served only to create more confusion for those trying to make sense of the geography of the West African interior. Some geographers, including Major James Rennell, the African Association's adviser on geographical matters, dismissed Shabeni's information as fabricated nonsense. However, within Shabeni's material there were some nuggets of excellent information, in particular his confident assertion that the Niger flowed into the sea.

Major Rennell, who had been Surveyor-General of Bengal from 1764 to 1777, was an accomplished cartographer and geographer, and a classical scholar of some distinction. In the 1790s he was engaged in a special study of the geography of Herodotus, and other writers of classical antiquity. His deep interest in classical antiquity profoundly influenced his approach to the study of African geography, leading him to an extreme reliance on the classical and ancient Arabic sources, and to a distrust of all contemporary information that could not be readily related to his interpretation of the classical and ancient sources, especially the works of al-Idrisi and Leo Africanus. In the absence of anything better, there was something to be said for this method, provided that the contemporary descriptions of routes, distances and physical features were detailed and very clear, but this was seldom the case. Another problem with his method was that it completely ignored historical change. The West African Empires of which al-Idrisi and Leo Africanus had written — Ghana, Mali, Songhai — had long since disintegrated, and some of the cities and towns they had named no longer existed, or could no longer be identified by the names they had used.

In October 1790 the African Association dispatched a third investigator to Africa. Major Daniel Houghton had visited Morocco in 1773 and had also served at the British fort on Gorée island, just off Dakar, between 1779–83. While at Gorée he had acquired some knowledge of the languages of the Senegambia. He approached the African Association with the suggestion that they appoint him to search for the Niger, from the trading posts along the Gambia River. The Association accepted his offer, commissioning him to search for the Niger, and to travel on to Timbuktu and Houssa. The reports of Lucas, the consuls in North Africa and Shabeni had brought the name Houssa to the attention of the European geographers. Their reports were interpreted as suggesting the existence of an empire, or a significant state of that name, lying to the east of Timbuktu.

Arriving in the Gambia, Houghton made contact with the British honorary consul, Dr John Laidley, who traded for slaves and ivory with the *slatees*, the African long-distance traders, from his factory at Pisania, several days journey up the Gambia river. Houghton set off for the interior travelling through the Mandingo states of Wuli, Bondu and Bambuk. From Bambuk he sent back information he had received relating to the Niger. His informant had told him that the river flowed from west to east, and that decked sailing ships carried goods past the city of Timbuktu towards the east. Houghton travelled on by a northerly route in the general direction of Timbuktu, passing through the African kingdoms of Khasso and Kaarta. From Simbing on the border of Kaarta with the Moorish kingdom of Ludamar, Houghton sent back a brief message to Dr Laidley, on 1 September 1791, to advise him that he was pressing on towards Timbuktu, notwithstanding the fact that he had been robbed of all his goods. This was the last that was ever heard from Houghton, though Dr Laidley later received reports that he was dead.

On receiving Houghton's information relating to the Niger, and the routes followed by the *slatees*, the African Association approached the British Government with the suggestion that a consul be appointed to reside in the Gambia for the purpose of developing a more extensive trade with the interior. The African Association had a candidate for the post of Consul on the Gambia, one James Willis. He was appointed Consul-General in April 1794 and arrangements were put in hand to send him out with fifty soldiers and a small armed ship. France and Britain were at war and Government may have seen the appointment of a Consul, with some armed force at his disposal, as a way of deterring any French moves against British interests on the Gambia. The proposed Gambia Consulate may also have been seen as a means towards extending British influence and trade in the region, at the expense of the French. However, Willis would be tied to a base on the Gambia, while the African Association needed someone prepared to follow in Houghton's footsteps, with all the risks that might entail. It was at this point that Mungo Park returned from Sumatra, eager for an appointment that promised adventure and the possibility of fame.

4

To the Gambia

On Mungo Park's return to London from Scotland in July 1794, he was interviewed by Sir Joseph Banks and Henry Beaufoy on behalf of the African Association. Though Mungo was only twenty-three years old and had relatively little experience, Banks and Beaufoy were satisfied that he was sufficiently qualified. No doubt they were impressed by his enthusiasm for travel in the cause of science, and his eagerness to undertake an exploration of the West African interior for the African Association. Mungo was appointed at the rate of 7s 6d a day from 1 August 1794 to the day of his departure from the Gambia for the Niger, plus £200 for outfit. From the day of his departure from the Gambia he would receive 15s 0d a day for up to two years spent in Africa.

The original plan was for Mungo Park to leave Britain with Consul Willis in September or October 1794. Willis experienced difficulties recruiting troops for service in the Gambia, and then other problems arose, with Willis demanding that a second ship be placed at his disposal. During this waiting period Mungo probably prepared himself for what he would find in West Africa, by reading the works of those English and French writers who had travelled in the Senegambia region. He also received what he later referred to as 'valuable Instructions' from Major Rennell, presumably relating to the recording and mapping of his journey. In November 1794 Mungo presented a paper to the Linnean Society, subsequently published in the Society's *Transactions*, in which he described in Latin eight fish species, all apparently new to science, that he had observed and recorded during the twelve weeks he had spent on the coast of Sumatra.

Early in 1795, tired of waiting for Willis to complete his arrangements, Mungo approached the Committee of the African Association, requesting that they send him out to the Gambia as soon as passage could be arranged. Probably because of the war with France and the activities of French privateers, this proved to be more difficult than might have been expected. However, Mungo did eventually secure passage with Captain Richard Wyatt, in the brig *Endeavour*, trading to the Gambia for ivory and beeswax, and left Portsmouth on 22 May 1795.

The *Endeavour* made an uneventful passage to the Gambia, where Mungo Park first set foot in Africa on 21 June 1795. Captain Wyatt used the tide to take the *Endeavour* up river to his destinations, the trading towns of Vintain and Jonkakonda, the latter a considerable distance up river from the sea. Mungo had a letter of introduction from Henry Beaufoy, secretary of the African Association, to Dr John Laidley, whose trading post at Pisania was not far from Jonkakonda. On receiving news of the arrival of the *Endeavour*, Dr Laidley came to Jonkakonda, and on meeting Mungo and receiving Beaufoy's letter, invited Mungo to stay with him until he was ready to set out for the Niger. This invitation Mungo was only too pleased to accept and on 5 July, provided with a guide and a horse by his host, Mungo made his way to Pisania, a place that had no existence save as a European slave trading station. In 1795 there were only three British traders — Dr Laidley and the brothers Ainsley — and their African dependants living there, under the protection of the local ruler.

Mungo Park's plan was to wait out the rainy season in expectation of the arrival of Willis, who never came, his mission having been postponed and later cancelled. Mungo intended to take instruction in the Mandingo language, learn what he could of the interior, and observe the country and its people. Laidley, who from long residence in the Gambia was fluent in Mandingo, found him language instructors. Mungo sought out the *slatees*, seeking information about the interior, but got very little from them. It quickly became clear to him that the *slatees* were suspicious of his plan to journey to the far interior and were most reluctant to have him join them when they left the Gambia.

On 31 July Mungo stayed out late to make observations of an eclipse of the moon and promptly went down with a severe bout of fever. At the

Erythrina
Senegalensis.
*Watercolour by
Mungo Park.
Sketched and painted
at Pisania, on the
Gambia River, 1795.*

time, it was widely believed that exposure to night-time dew was the cause
of the fevers that often killed new arrivals from Europe. Mungo made a
slow recovery, being confined to the house for most of August, and
suffering a relapse in September. Recovering from what was almost
certainly malaria, Mungo gained a certain degree of resistance to and
immunity from further attacks. Without this 'seasoning' experience, as it
was known to Europeans resident in West Africa, Mungo would have been
at great risk over the next few months. He certainly suffered several more
attacks of fever over the next two years of travel but survived them all.

While staying at Pisania, and particularly during his convalescence,
Mungo engaged in some botanical study, sketching and making
watercolours of some of the plants found in the area. A sketchbook
containing drawings and watercolours he made at this time is now to be
found in the Library of the Royal Botanic Garden, Edinburgh.

Mungo observed that Islam had made significant progress among the peoples of the Senegambia region, including the Mandingo, who were dominant on the Gambia river, and in most of the country through which he would subsequently travel. Islam in this part of West Africa had developed and extended its influence as a result of the trading contacts that had long existed between the region and the Maghreb. Muslim merchants from Morocco and other parts of North Africa settled in trading centres, where they acted as informal missionaries, gained converts and in some states in the region secured a limited influence in the courts of the local rulers, who generally continued to follow traditional religious practices.

The institutions of government that Mungo Park observed in the Mandingo states of the region typically took the form of limited monarchy. In all important matters the rulers would call assemblies of the leading men, or elders. The rulers generally acted on the advice of these assemblies, and were dependent upon their consent for a decision to declare war, or conclude peace. Local administration, including the administration of justice, was in the hands of hereditary magistrates known as *alkaid* (*qadi* judge). It was their task to keep order, levy duties on travellers and preside over administrative councils and judicial courts. These courts, which Mungo frequently attended as an observer, were composed of the free elders of the town, meeting in public. Mungo observed both gravity and decorum in the proceedings of these courts, both sides to a case being free to argue their cause, witnesses being publicly examined and the decisions taken generally receiving the approval of the onlookers.

The basis for judgements in the courts was ancient custom but this was being partly overlaid by recourse to the *shari'a*, or Islamic canon law, a result of the presence of an increasing number of Muslims in the community and the availability of a written code to which reference could be made. Muslim jurists in West Africa were prepared to allow for the application of local customary law, and in practice the *alkaid* took his decisions in the light of both *shari'a* and customary law and the prevailing social realities.

As Mungo Park observed, the recourse to written law in the form of the *shari'a*, with which those following traditional religious practices were entirely unacquainted, had given rise to the emergence of a class of advocates who attended the court and pleaded for plaintiff or defendant in much the same manner as did counsel in the British courts:

> They are Mahomedan Negroes who have made, or effect to have made the laws of the Prophet their peculiar study; and if I may judge from their harangues, which I frequently attended, I believe that in the forensic qualifications of procrastination and cavil, and the arts of confounding and perplexing a cause, they are not always surpassed by the ablest pleaders in Europe.

Mungo Park paid considerable attention during his stay in the Gambia to the institution of slavery, and also to the slave trade. He noted that perhaps one quarter of the population were free men and women, the rest being bound in a condition of hereditary slavery, and employed in cultivation, the care of livestock and in servile offices of all kinds. Islamic law and customary law imposed restrictions on what a master could do with a hereditary slave, and gave the slave certain limited rights. In principle the slave could not be deprived of life, or sold to a stranger, without a public trial. The treatment of slaves taken in war, or sold into slavery for crimes or insolvency, was altogether different. Brought from the interior by the *slatees*, they had no protection from the law and the owner could do with them whatever he wished. The *slatees* would hope to make a quick sale to the European slave-traders, but if there were no slave ships on the river, the slaves would be distributed around the neighbouring villages, where they would be held in fetters, employed to labour in the fields, poorly fed and harshly treated. Mungo noted that while the price of slaves was variable, depending on demand and supply, a young healthy male aged sixteen to twenty-five might sell for eighteen to twenty pounds sterling.

The European slave trade on the Gambia river at the time of Mungo Park's visit was much reduced from what it had been in the first half of the eighteenth century, when the English and French were in vigorous competition. Mungo was informed that less than 1,000 slaves were being exported annually from the Gambia, with only two or three English slave ships expected each year, plus an occasional French, Danish or American ship. Slaves remained the chief object of European commercial interest in the Gambia but gold dust, ivory, beeswax and hides were also sought.

The most significant items in the European exports to the Gambia were guns and ammunition, followed by ironware, spirits, tobacco, cotton goods and trifles such as glass beads and amber. Guns and ammunition were taken to the interior by the *slatees* who sold them to the slave-raiding rulers, who then sold the slaves they captured to the *slatees*, so as to buy more guns and ammunition, wherewith to raid for more slaves.... The *slatees* also supplied the population of the Gambia region with various commodities from the interior, including shea-butter, a substance extracted from the kernel of the fruit of the shea-nut tree (*Butyrospermum paradoxum, s.s. Parki*), which was used as a substitute for butter, and for every domestic purpose for which oil was used. Mungo Park observed the preparation of shea-butter in the interior, and brought the tree and its product to the notice of the European scientific community.

During the month of October the rains slackened, the level of the river fell rapidly and the *slatees* made preparations to leave for the interior. Mungo, now recovered from the fever, also started to make preparations for departure. It had been his intention to join a large caravan proceeding inland, but finding the *slatees* suspicious of his plans and unwilling to enter into an agreement with him, he resolved to make the journey with an interpreter and one servant, both found for him by Dr Laidley. These two were Johnson, hired as an interpreter, and a boy, Demba, whom Mungo engaged as a servant. Demba was one of Dr Laidley's slaves, who was promised his freedom if he acquitted himself well during the journey. Johnson had been a slave in the West Indies and as a free man had lived for many years in England, before returning home to the Gambia. He was fluent in English and Mandingo, while Demba spoke both Mandingo and the language of the Serahuli people.

Mungo purchased a horse for himself and two asses for Johnson and Demba, packed his few belongings, provisions for a few days, and some trade goods — beads, amber and tobacco — for the purchase of fresh supplies of foodstuffs. Four others joined Mungo's little party, two Serahuli *slatees* on their way to Bondu; Tami, a blacksmith, who had been employed by Dr Laidley, and was returning to his village in Khasso; and another man travelling to the Bambara kingdom of Segu, all on foot and driving loaded asses. They left Pisania on 2 December 1795, escorted by Dr Laidley and the brothers Ainsley, who remained with them until the early afternoon of the next day, when they separated. As Mungo rode off into the woods, his thoughts turned to what he imagined might lie before him:

> a boundless forest, and a country, the inhabitants of which were strangers to civilised life, and to most of whom a white man was the object of curiosity or plunder. I reflected that I had parted from the last European I might probably behold, and perhaps quitted for ever the comforts of Christian society.

He was soon roused from these despondent thoughts by the arrival of a large body of people demanding a customs payment on behalf of the king of Walli. Mungo considered it prudent to comply with their demands and handed over some tobacco. The party was then allowed to proceed, and the following day passed into the kingdom of Wuli. On arrival at Medina, the capital of Wuli, Mungo attended on the king to pay his respects, and to obtain permission to pass through his country to Bondu. The king, who had welcomed Major Houghton, was equally obliging to Mungo Park and provided him with a guide to the border. The king tried to persuade Mungo to abandon his journey to the interior, observing that if he continued he would probably meet the same fate as that which had befallen Major Houghton. When Mungo made it clear that he was resolved to go on, the king assured him he would pray for his safe return.

Near to the entrance of the town of Kolor, Mungo observed a masquerade costume made of bark, hanging from a tree. He was told that this belonged to Mumbo Jumbo, a masquerade employed in a ceremony designed to keep women in subjection. In the polygamous households of the Mandingo towns, the quarrels between wives sometimes destroyed household peace and undermined the authority of the male household head. In such cases Mumbo Jumbo was called upon and his intervention was invariably decisive. The masquerade, who might be the husband, or someone instructed by him, would announce his evening visitation by shrieks and howls from the woods close by the town. When it was dark, clad in the bark costume, and carrying a staff or scourge, the masquerade entered the town and proceeded to the *bentang* (a public meeting place, usually under a large tree and in the centre of the town), where all the inhabitants would assemble. The married women had no idea who was to be the subject of Mumbo's attention, so each one feared that his visitation might be for herself. The women dared not absent themselves, and were obliged to spend the evening singing and dancing until around midnight...

about which time Mumbo fixes on the offender. This unfortunate victim being thereupon immediately seized, is stripped naked, tied to a post, and severely scourged with Mumbo's rod, amidst the shouts and derision of the whole assembly; and it is remarkable, that the rest of the women are loudest in their exclamations on this occasion against their unhappy sister. Daylight puts an end to this indecent and unmanly revel.

The guide supplied by the king of Wuli, having taken Mungo's party to the border, now left them, and Mungo hired elephant hunters as guides to take them through the wilderness that separated Wuli from Bondu, a two-day journey through an area said to be frequented by bandits, and where water was scarce. The journey through the wilderness was uneventful, though Mungo's companions remained apprehensive of attack until they reached Tallika, the border town of Bondu.

5

From Bondu to Kaarta

Bondu, though a small state and tributary to the kingdom of Kaarta, some distance away to the east, was prosperous and growing in strength, having recently taken territory from its eastern neighbour Bambuk. Important trade routes ran through the state and heavy duties were levied on goods passing through. In fertile Bondu many Fulah nomads had settled and were engaged in cultivation as well as the pasture of cattle. Mandingo and Serahuli farmers and traders were settled in Bondu in some numbers, as the state had become a refuge for people in flight from the warfare and raiding that characterised many of the neighbouring states.

Bondu was well on the way to becoming a Muslim state at the time of Mungo Park's visit, though the king remained a pagan. The majority of the inhabitants were Muslims and Islamic law was widely observed. As Mungo travelled through Bondu he saw many little schools where the children of both Muslim and pagan parents were taught to read the Koran and given instruction in the principles of Islam. As he observed, it was by means of these schools that the Islamic religion had become firmly established in Bondu.

Passing through hilly country the party reached a tributary of the Senegal river, the swiftly flowing Falemé, which they crossed, arriving at Fatteconda, the capital of Bondu. Here Mungo was summoned to meet the ruler, the Almami Amadi Isata. Mungo explained himself and his reasons for travelling through Bondu. The Almami seemed surprised that

Mungo had not come to trade for slaves or gold, but invited Mungo to visit him at his residence that same evening, when he would supply him with provisions. Mungo was suspicious of the Almami's intentions towards him, having learnt that he had ill-treated Major Houghton. Mungo deemed it politic to attend on the Almami with suitable presents, so took with him some gunpowder, amber, tobacco and his umbrella, intending these as gifts. He thought it likely that his lodgings would be searched during his absence, so concealed some articles in the roof of hut in which he lodged, and wore his best blue coat in the hope that this might preserve it from thieves.

When Mungo attended on the Almami that evening, he again explained the object of his journey and reasons for passing through Bondu. The Almami was astonished that anyone should undertake such a dangerous journey merely to observe the country and its inhabitants. After Mungo had displayed his few possessions, the Almami was satisfied that he did not come as a trader and accepted his presents, expressing particular pleasure in the umbrella. The Almami then began to praise the Europeans, extolling them for their wealth and generous disposition, all this being no more than a preamble to a request for Mungo's coat.

> The request of an African prince, in his own dominions, particularly when made to a stranger, comes little short of a command. It is only a way of obtaining by gentle means what he can, if he pleases, take by force; and as it was against my interest to offend him by a refusal, I very quickly took off my coat, the only good one in my possession, and laid it at his feet.

The Almami responded with a generous supply of provisions and asked Mungo to visit him the following morning, when Mungo found him in bed and unwell. He asked Mungo to draw some blood, which he agreed to do. However, when all was ready and Mungo produced the lancet, the Almami changed his mind and begged Mungo to postpone the operation until the afternoon. He told Mungo that his women had expressed a desire to see the stranger, and had him escorted to the seraglio. A dozen ladies, most of them young and well-favoured, instantly surrounded Mungo, begging for physic or amber, and all of them eager to have their veins opened by the young *hakim* (physician). Mungo does

45

not record whether he performed the operation on any of the ladies, but some good-natured banter ensued during the visit, the ladies chaffing him on his unnatural appearance, while he extolled African beauty. They called him *honey-mouth*, a flatterer, and on his departure presented him with some fish and a jar of honey. That same evening Mungo again visited the Almami, to seek his permission to leave Bondu, taking with him a small leave-taking present. In return the king gave him a small quantity of gold-dust, saying that it would be useful for the purchase of provisions on the journey, and told Mungo that he was at liberty to leave whenever he wished.

Leaving Fatteconda on the following day, Mungo and his party travelled in a north-easterly direction, toward the Serahuli state of Kajaaga, but before they could reach it they had to cross a wilderness area, reported to be dangerous for travellers and best crossed at night. Mungo agreed to this and hired guides to take the party through the area. Nothing happened on the march through this wilderness, though the party was shadowed by hyenas, and the creatures Mungo refers to as wolves — probably African wild dogs. Arriving in the town of Joag, Mungo and his party lodged with the headman, here known as the *dooty*, who treated them hospitably.

Kajaaga was at this time an independent state, or confederacy of small chiefdoms, on the brink of war with its eastern neighbour Khasso. The Serahuli people, also known as Soninke, were great traders who had played a key role in the ancient salt and gold trade, and remained active in that trade as well as in the slave and ivory trades. They were widely dispersed, and were known by other names — notably Dyula and Wangara — in different parts of West Africa. They were among the first of the peoples of West Africa to have come into regular contact with Arabs and Berbers from North Africa who settled in the Soninke state of Ancient Ghana, where there were mosques and Muslim advisers to the pagan ruler in the eleventh century AD.

Joag was a substantial walled town with perhaps 2,000 inhabitants and it was here that Mungo Park had his first really unpleasant experience. Mungo, his attendants and travelling companions were apprehended by a group of twenty armed horsemen, led by the local king's son. Mungo asked their leader to address him in Mandingo, and not in Serahuli, a language he did not understand. This he agreed to do, and informed

A mosque and bentang *in Kajaaga (Galam).*

Mungo that as he had entered the town without having paid the customary duties, or having given a present to the *Batcheri,* the ruler of Kajaaga, all Mungo's people, animals and baggage were forfeit. Mungo's travelling companions were terrified, particularly the blacksmith, who as a native of Khasso feared not only the loss of all his savings but enslavement. The leader then told Mungo that he was ordered to bring him and all his party to the *Batcheri,* by force if necessary. Resistance was useless, but Mungo sought to buy some time by saying that he needed to feed his horse and settle matters with the *dooty,* his landlord. He consulted the *dooty,* who advised him not to accompany these men if he could possibly avoid doing so. Mungo then offered the leader all the gold he had received from the Almami of Bondu, as a present for the *Batcheri.* The gold was accepted and the horsemen left, but not before searching Mungo's baggage and taking half his remaining goods, apart from some few items he had concealed.

Shortly after this incident, Mungo received news that the nephew of the ruler of Khasso, Demba Sego Jalla, was on his way to see him. This young man, who bore the same name as his uncle, had been on an unsuccessful mission to the *Batcheri,* ruler of Kajaaga, to try and settle the differences between the two states. Hearing that a white man was at Joag,

47

curiosity brought him to see Mungo. On learning of their misfortunes, the young man offered to escort Mungo and his companions to Khasso, and to be responsible for their safety on the journey. Mungo gratefully accepted this offer and the following day the party left Joag and reached the Senegal river, which formed the boundary between Kajaaga and Khasso.

Immediately upon arrival in Khasso, Demba Sego made it clear to Mungo that he expected a generous present for having brought him out of danger in Kajaaga. Since the young man knew that Mungo had lost a large proportion of his goods at Joag, this came as an unwelcome and unexpected request, leading Mungo to wonder whether he had improved his situation much. He realised that it would be pointless to complain and gave Demba Sego some amber and tobacco, which appeared to satisfy him.

The party made a long day's march from the Senegal river to the town of Teesee, where Tiggity Sego, brother of the king, and Demba Sego's father, was the chief. Tiggity Sego was curious to know why Mungo was exploring the country, and he clearly doubted Mungo's explanation, apparently believing that Mungo had some secret purpose. He told Mungo that it would be necessary for him to travel to the town of Kooniakary, to pay his respects to the king, his brother. Demba Sego was appointed to undertake a mission to the Moorish state of Gedumah (Guidimaka) to the north-west of Khasso, and he borrowed Mungo's horse, promising to return it after three days. Nine days later he returned and Mungo, annoyed at the delay, immediately sought Tiggity Sego's permission to proceed to Kooniakary, the residence of Demba Sego Jalla. Permission was refused until such time as Mungo paid the usual dues Tiggity Sego was entitled to receive from travellers, with some addition for his 'kindness' to Mungo. The following day Demba Sego and some companions came to collect what Mungo felt able to offer from his much diminished supply of trade goods. Demba Sego told Mungo that the present he had prepared was inadequate, adding that he would take all Mungo's goods to his father and let him choose what he wanted. He did not execute this threat, but instead made a thorough search of all Mungo's bundles and took whatever he and his companions fancied, leaving half of what little remained.

Leaving Teesee on 10 January 1796, Mungo and his party travelled to Jumbo, the hometown of Tami, the blacksmith who had accompanied

Mungo from Pisania. Nearing the town, they were met by Tami's brother, and a praise-singer, with others. A joyful crowd welcomed the blacksmith and escorted him to his family home. Mungo witnessed Tami's emotional reunion with his family, an affecting moment that Mungo described when he came to write of his experiences in Africa:

> the blacksmith's aged mother was led forth leaning upon a staff. Everyone made way for her; and she stretched out her hand to bid her son welcome. Being totally blind, she stroked his hands, arms and face with great care, and seemed highly delighted that her later days were blessed by his return, and that her ears once more heard the music of his voice. From this interview I was fully convinced that whatever difference there is between the Negro and the European in the conformation of the nose and the colour of the skin, there is none in the genuine sympathies and characteristic feelings of our common nature.

Mungo and his attendants joined in the celebration of Tami's return and remained in the town for three days. Accompanied by Tami, who was sincerely grateful to Mungo for his protection on the journey, the party left for Koonikary on 14 January, making a diversion to the village of Soolo in order to meet Salim Daucari, a *slatee*, who had received credit from Dr Laidley. Mungo had an order from Dr Laidley for the whole value of the debt, approximately 100 pounds sterling. Fortunately, Salim Daucari was at home and he welcomed Mungo and undertook to provide him with whatever funds he could raise.

Demba Sego Jalla, the king of Khasso, also welcomed Mungo, accepted his reasons for travelling through the country and promised such assistance as he could give. At a later audience with the king, Mungo learnt that further progress to the east might be prevented by war, as the Bambara state of Segu was making preparations to invade Khasso's eastern neighbour Kaarta. The king suggested that Mungo should wait, while he sent to Kaarta for information on the situation. Mungo agreed and returned to Soolo to lodge with Salim Daucari, while waiting for news from Kaarta.

When Salim Daucari had supplied Mungo with gold dust and some trade goods to the value of sixty pounds, Mungo appealed to the king to allow him to leave by a south-easterly route through Fooladoo. The king's reply was that Mungo could leave by that route if he wished, but that he could not undertake to provide him with a guide, since he was obliged by treaty to send all traders and travellers to the east, through Kaarta. Mungo, warned by his experiences in Kajaaga, where he had had no guide and no safe-conduct from the ruler, accepted the king's advice, and resigned himself to waiting until news came from Kaarta.

Sambo Sego, the king's son, having learnt that Mungo was now well provided with funds, rode over to visit him, accompanied by several followers. He demanded to know how much Mungo had received and insisted that half of it must be paid to the king, with additional presents to himself and his companions. Mungo knew that this was extortion but was prepared to submit 'thinking it was highly dangerous to make a foolish resistance, and irritate the lion when within reach of his paw'. Salim Daucari, Mungo's host, realised what was going on and intervened on his guest's behalf, persuading Sambo to accept a modest present as a complete discharge of Mungo's obligations in Khasso.

On 1 February news came from Kaarta that the war had not yet begun and that it might be possible for Mungo to pass through the country before the invasion of the Segu army commenced. Two days later, after taking leave of Salim Daucari and Tami, Mungo left Soolo for Kaarta with his attendants and two guides appointed by the king of Khasso. On their way they encountered hundreds of refugees in flight from the impending war in Kaarta, which they entered on 9 February.

On arrival in Kemmoo, the capital of Kaarta, Mungo was received by the king, whom he names as Daisy Koorabarri (better rendered as Desse Kouliballi). Mungo explained his reasons for travelling to Kaarta, and for seeking a safe-conduct for onward travel to Segu. The king seemed perfectly satisfied with Mungo's explanation of his journey, but told him that as communication with Segu had been interrupted for some time, and the Segu army would soon invade Kaarta, Mungo could not safely travel by the usual routes. If he attempted it, he would very likely be taken for a spy and killed. The king could not accept that Mungo should remain in Kaarta, lest some accident befall him in the impending war, in which case he and his people might be blamed for his death. He advised Mungo to return to Khasso and wait for the war to come to an end, which would probably be in three or four months' time. This was good advice but

Mungo, aware that the hot weather was coming, and that the rains, which he dreaded, would soon follow, pleaded with the king to give him a guide to any other part of the borders of Kaarta from which he might journey to Segu. The king acknowledged that one route remained open, adding that it was not without danger. This route would take Mungo to the north-east, into the Moorish kingdom of Ludamar, from where it would be possible to enter Segu by a circuitous route. While this was being discussed, a messenger arrived with important news for the king. The king gave a sign for strangers to leave, which Mungo promptly did. However, he soon learnt that the messenger had informed the king that the Segu army was on the move, and on the point of invading Kaarta.

The following day, 13 February, Mungo sent his pistols to the king as a present, with the request that the king provide him with a guide for Ludamar, as soon as convenient. The king thanked Mungo for his present and appointed an escort to take him to the border town of Jarra, advising him to leave as soon as possible, so that his men might return before battle was joined with the Segu army. A few hours later Mungo, his attendants and the escort left Kemmoo.

6

From Kaarta to Ludamar — capture and humiliation

Two days after leaving Kemmoo, Mungo and his party halted at the town of Funingkedy, where he was informed that Moors were raiding in the area and driving away cattle. From the town, Mungo witnessed a raid by a small party of Moors, who drove off sixteen cattle, encountering little opposition. One young herdsman had offered resistance and had been shot by a Moor, the musket ball passing through his leg and breaking both bones below the knee. Mungo, who was asked to examine the young man, who had lost a lot of blood, advised that the only hope for recovery and that a slender one, was amputation above the knee. This horrified the man's friends and relatives, who had never heard of such a method of treatment and would not consent to it. The young man was placed in the care of some Muslim elders, who whispered to him in Arabic, desiring him to repeat what they had said, namely the first words of the *shahada*, the confession of faith, which he eventually managed to do. The elders now assured his distraught mother that her son would be happy in the after life. The young man died later that day.

Mungo's guides advised him that it would be best to travel by night, on account of the Moorish raiders in the area; so with a group of refugees from Kaarta, who were heading for Ludamar to escape the war, they made a night march to Simbing, the frontier village where Major Houghton had written his last letter to Dr Laidley. Mungo later learnt that several Moorish merchants had tricked the Major into accompanying them into the desert, where they robbed him of what little he had left and then abandoned him. He was starving, but on foot he managed to find his way to some wells. The Moors at the wells refused to give him any food, and he either died from starvation and exhaustion, or was murdered.

On 18 February, Mungo's party arrived at Jarra, a substantial town on the southern boundary of Ludamar, one of several Moorish states established as a result of the migration of Berber and Arab nomads into the northern margins of the savannah of West Africa, to the north and east of the Senegal river and towards the Middle Niger, a process that had been going on for centuries. The indigenous black African populations of these areas were either displaced or reduced to the status of a subject population.

At Jarra, Mungo obtained lodgings at the house of Daman Jumma, a *slatee*, who had received goods on credit from Dr Laidley. Mungo had an order from Dr Laidley for the whole value of the debt, the equivalent of six slaves. Daman Jumma acknowledged the debt, regretting that as things were with him at that time, he could only make a payment to the value of two slaves. However, he was able to exchange Mungo's remaining beads and amber for gold, more portable and more easily concealed.

Mungo's attendants, Johnson and Demba, were frightened by the situation in which they found themselves, fearful of being seized and enslaved by the Moors, and they told Mungo they would not accompany him further toward the east. Mungo understood their fears and was prepared to let them return to the Gambia, but was resolved to continue his journey. He secured Daman Jumma's help in making an approach to Ali, the ruler of Ludamar for permission to pass unmolested through his country, to the border with Segu. After fourteen days, one of Ali's slaves arrived with instructions to escort Mungo to the border. Demba now came to Mungo and told him that he had never had any intention of deserting him, but had joined with Johnson in the hope that their combined refusal to continue would persuade him to return to the Gambia. Mungo prepared to depart with Demba and a slave of Daman Jumma's who he had hired as a guide. He bade farewell to Johnson who intended to return to the Gambia when an opportunity presented itself.

On 27 February the party left Jarra and, travelling through dry and sandy country, after two days reached the town of Deena, where Mungo was subjected to insult at the hands of some Moors who spat in his face with a view to provoking him to retaliation, thus affording a pretext for further ill-treatment. When this failed, they resorted to what they regarded as a perfect justification for robbery, namely that since the traveller was a Christian, his property was lawful plunder for Muslims. They seized Mungo's baggage and took whatever they fancied from it. Mungo's attendants, observing that anyone could rob him with impunity, were now determined to return to Jarra. Mungo tried to persuade them to continue with him, but they would not listen, and fearing some further insult from the Moors, he resolved to leave on his own. He left Deena in the early hours of the morning of 3 March, but had not gone far when Demba came after him and told him that as the Moors had left, he thought he could persuade the guide to join them. Mungo waited while Demba returned to Deena, and after a short time returned with the guide.

For several days Mungo's party journeyed on toward the east, passing through several towns and villages largely inhabited by black Africans, and in these places they were hospitably received and entertained. Mungo now thought that he was out of danger from the Moors and his imagination had already placed him on the banks of the Niger. He felt able to relax and may have slowed the pace of the march. On 7 March, at a village only two days journey from the border, while Mungo was conversing and drinking with the *dooty* and his friends, a party of Moors made an appearance:

> They came, they said by Ali's orders, to convey me to his camp at Benowm. If I went peaceably, they told me I had nothing to fear: but if I refused, they had orders, to bring me by force. I was struck dumb with surprise and terror, which the Moors observing, endeavoured to calm my apprehensions by repeating the assurance that I had nothing to fear.

The Moors told Mungo that Ali required his presence in order to satisfy the curiosity of his wife, Fatima, who having heard much of Christians was anxious to see one. They said that when her curiosity was satisfied, Ali would allow him to depart and provide him with an escort to Segu. Mungo did not trust these assurances but there was nothing he could do, and with Demba, he was taken to Ali's camp at Benowm, the two of them kept under close guard at night. Arriving at Benowm, a large encampment of dirty-looking tents, Mungo was led into Ali's presence, through a crowd whose curiosity was of an insulting and somewhat threatening nature. Ali was an old man of Arab appearance, with a long white beard and a sullen countenance. He looked Mungo over and inquired as to whether he spoke Arabic. He appeared surprised at the negative answer and lapsed into silence. When it was time for the evening prayer, the Moorish interpreter told Mungo that Ali was about to present him with something to eat, and looking round Mungo observed some boys bringing in a live wild hog. Ali then made signs to Mungo that he should kill and prepare it for his evening meal. Though very hungry, Mungo thought it wise not to kill and eat an animal so much abhorred by the Moors, and told Ali that he never ate such food. This was not the end of Ali's attempt to have some sport with the hog at Mungo's expense, for the creature was cut loose in the expectation that it would immediately attack Mungo, the Moors believing that a state of great enmity existed between hogs and Christians. The hog attacked whoever got in its way, eventually taking shelter underneath the sofa on which Ali was seated. After this unpleasant farce, Mungo was led to the tent of Ali's chief slave, which he was not allowed to enter, but he was given a little food, and outside the tent a mat was placed on which he spent the night surrounded by a curious multitude.

The next morning Ali appeared and had Mungo conducted to a hut he had provided for him, constructed of corn stalks. The hut did provide some protection from the sun but there was an unwelcome occupant — the hog, tethered to one of the roof supports. The hog had been placed in the hut on Ali's order, an insulting and derisive gesture of contempt for the Christian. The presence of the hog was a great trial to Mungo as it drew the boys of the camp to his hut, where they would beat it with sticks until it was so enraged that it ran and bit at anyone it could reach. Mungo also had adult visitors, who insisted that he remove most of his clothes, so that they could inspect them, and observe the way in which he dressed and undressed himself. This went on for hours, from noon until evening, when some food was brought to the prisoner. That same night, an intruder, perhaps intent on theft, stumbled over Demba and fell on top of the hog, which promptly bit him. His screams roused the people, including Ali, who assumed Mungo had been trying to escape. In due course order was restored and Mungo and Demba were allowed to sleep.

The next day the same wearisome round commenced, the boys coming to beat the hog, the adults to plague the Christian. When Mungo came to record his experiences in Ludamar, he wrote of his period as Ali's prisoner:

> It is impossible for me to describe the behaviour of a people who study mischief as a science, and exult in the miseries and misfortunes of their fellow-creatures. It is sufficient to observe that the rudeness, ferocity and fanaticism, which distinguish the Moors from the rest of mankind, found here a proper subject whereon to exercise their propensities. I was a *stranger*, I was *unprotected*, and I was a *Christian*; each of these circumstances is sufficient to drive every spark of humanity from the heart of a Moor; but when all of them, as in my case, were combined in the same person, and a suspicion prevailed withal, that I had come as a *spy* into the country, the reader will easily imagine that I had every thing to fear.

Ali had sent some of his people to Jarra to fetch Johnson, and any property of Mungo's that might have been left there. Ali questioned Johnson, and then had Mungo brought to him to explain the contents of a bundle of clothes he had left at Jarra, should he return that way. Later that day, Ali had all Mungo's baggage removed to his tent 'for safe keeping'. He was disappointed to find only a small quantity of gold and amber in Mungo's baggage, and the next day he had Mungo rudely searched, and his watch and all the gold and amber he had concealed were taken. A compass was also taken but later returned, when Ali became convinced that it had magical properties and might be dangerous to him.

On 20 March, Ali and some of the chief men debated Mungo's fate. According to what Mungo was told by different people, some wanted him put to death, others were for cutting off his right hand. One of Ali's sons, a boy of about nine years of age, told Mungo that his uncle had persuaded his father to have Mungo blinded, and that the assembly had agreed to this. However, Ali had decided to postpone execution of this sentence until Fatima, his wife, had seen the Christian.

Mungo suffered an attack of fever in March and tried to make his persecutors understand that he was sick and needed sleep. They understood well enough, but as he observed:

my distress was a matter of sport to them, and they endeavoured to heighten it by every means in their power. This studied and degrading insolence, to which I was constantly exposed, was one of the bitterest ingredients in the cup of captivity, and often made life itself a burden to me.

One day, while he was still feverish, he tried to escape his tormentors by wandering off to a group of trees that stood just outside the camp, where he lay down to try and get some rest. Peace and solitude was too great an indulgence for the despised Christian and one of Ali's sons, with others, rode over to force him back into the camp. Mungo was brought before Ali, who sternly informed him that if he were seen outside the camp again, without having obtained permission, he would be shot.

Mungo had been much troubled by the curiosity of the Moorish women from the day of his arrival in Benowm, and on 25 March this curiosity took a somewhat unexpected turn. A group of women came to his hut and gave him to understand that they wished to ascertain by inspection whether or not he was circumcised:

The reader will judge of my surprise at this unexpected declaration; and in order to avoid the proposed scrutiny, I thought it best to treat the business jocularly. I observed to them, that it was not customary in my country to give ocular demonstration in such cases, before so many beautiful women; but that if all of them would retire, except the young lady to whom I pointed (selecting the youngest and handsomest), I would satisfy her curiosity. The ladies enjoyed the jest, and went away laughing heartily; and the young damsel herself to whom I had given the preference (though she did not avail herself of the privilege of inspection), seemed no way displeased at the compliment, for she soon after sent me some meal and milk for my supper.

Toward the end of April the war in Kaarta threatened to spill over into Ludamar. Nominally, Ali was in alliance with Mansong, the king of Segu, against Kaarta, but Ali had done nothing to support him. Mansong sent to Ali requesting that his ally send a troop of horsemen to aid him. Ali refused the request and treated Mansong's messengers with contempt.

Mansong thereupon lifted his siege of the town of Gedingooma, a stronghold in the hill country of Kaarta, to which place Desse Kouliballi, the king of Kaarta, had withdrawn at an early stage of the war. Mansong was enraged by Ali's behaviour and marched his army north with the intention of invading Ludamar and punishing Ali. On learning of the advance of the Segu army toward Ludamar, Ali withdrew from Benowm northwards, toward the desert. When Mansong discovered that Ali and his people had left Benowm, he abandoned his intention of invading Ludamar, and the campaign against Kaarta, and returned to Segu.

Mungo and his attendants were among those evacuated from Benowm to Ali's new camp, near the town of Bubaker. On arrival at the camp, Mungo immediately waited upon Ali, to pay his respects to him, and to Fatima, who had now joined him. For the first and only time, Ali seemed pleased to see Mungo, shook his hand and introduced him to Fatima, a large lady of Arab appearance. Though initially she seemed shocked at finding a Christian in her presence, she relaxed after a while, and through an interpreter asked Mungo many questions about his country.

The heat was now at its most intense in this arid country with its sparse vegetation. Water was scarce and day and night the cattle crowded round the wells, lowing and fighting to get to the troughs into which men and boys poured what they raised from the wells. The scarcity of water was felt by everyone in the camp, and by none more than Mungo and his companions. Ali had supplied Mungo with a skin to contain water, and Fatima occasionally supplied a small quantity, when Mungo was in a distressed condition, but for a daily supply the captives depended on what they could get at the wells, or what they could beg.

Tormented by thirst, Mungo found himself dreaming of the Yarrow Water and other rivers of his homeland, surveying those clear and cooling streams with delight and anticipation; 'but alas! disappointment awakened me, and I found myself a lonely captive, perishing of thirst, amidst the wilds of Africa.' One night, having failed to beg any water in the camp, and in a feverish state, Mungo set off for the wells, about half a mile distant, where he found the Moors busy drawing water:

> I requested permission to drink, but was driven away with outrageous abuse. Passing, however, from one well to another, I came at last to

one where there was only an old man and two boys. I made the same request to this man, and he immediately drew me up a bucket of water; but as I was about to take hold of it, he recollected that I was a Christian, and fearing that his bucket might be polluted by my lips, he dashed the water into the trough and told me to drink from there. Though this trough was none of the largest and three cows were already drinking in it, I resolved to come in for my share; and kneeling down, thrust my head between two of the cows, and drank with great pleasure, until the water was nearly exhausted, and the cows began to contend with each other for the last mouthful.

As the month of May advanced it was obvious from the gathering clouds and the distant lightening that the rains were about to start. In this season, the Moors would move off to the north into the desert margins, and Mungo was apprehensive that with their departure his fate would be decided. Ali regarded Mungo as a prisoner, while Fatima, though apparently well disposed towards him, had said nothing about release. However, unexpected developments arising from the recent war in Kaarta, and the presence in Ludamar of a significant body of rebels against the authority of Desse Kouliballi, produced a situation that Mungo thought might be advantageous to him. The Kaarta rebels offered to treat with Ali for military assistance, in an offensive they intended to launch against Desse Kouliballi. The rebels knew that Desse Kouliballi would not allow them to return to their homes in peace, but would treat them as traitors and hunt them down. Furthermore, they could expect no security in the border areas of the neighbouring states, as Desse Kouliballi was likely to raid across the ill-defined and porous frontiers in pursuit of them. Ali saw an opportunity for extortion from these Kaarta rebels, who were desperate for his assistance, and sent one of his sons to Jarra to talk to them, preparing to follow in a few days time. Mungo saw this as presenting an opportunity for escape, and immediately applied to Fatima, begging her to intercede with Ali to grant him permission to accompany Ali to Jarra. This she did, and after some hesitation Ali agreed. Most of the clothing that had been taken from Mungo, his horse, saddle and bridle were restored to him, and together with Demba and Johnson he left Bubaker on 26 May, escorted by several Moors, meeting Ali and his party on the way to Jarra. Two days after leaving Bubaker, Ali's chief slave came and seized

Demba, telling him that Ali was now his master, and that he would be returned to Bubaker. Mungo was outraged at this treatment of his faithful servant and hastened to Ali to protest. Ali turned to Mungo 'with a haughty and malignant smile' and told him that if he did not immediately mount his horse, he too would be sent back to Bubaker. Mungo realised that there was nothing he could do for Demba, but did promise him that he would do his utmost to redeem him. Mungo had a real affection for Demba, who was not only loyal, but also a cheerful and willing servant. Demba seems to have been strongly attached to Mungo, and when they shook hands on parting, both of them were in tears.

Arriving at Jarra on 1 June, Mungo obtained lodgings with Daman Jumma, who had been his landlord when he had been at Jarra in February. He gave Daman Jumma an account of what had happened since his departure, and urgently requested him to use such influence as he had with Ali to redeem Demba. However, Ali would not agree to redemption, as he did not wish to see Demba reunited with Mungo, to act as his interpreter and companion on the way to Segu. Ali did indicate that he would be willing to sell Demba to Daman Jumma for his own use, for the ordinary price of a slave, at some future date.

Ali's business in Jarra was the extortion of cattle and goods from the Kaarta rebels, and the people of the town. Ali promised to support the rebels and agreed to hire out to them 200 of his cavalrymen to serve as mercenaries in any attempt they might make to overthrow Desse Kouliballi. Ali's price for the hire of his men was 400 head of cattle and other goods. Since the Kaarta rebels could not meet this price, they asked Ali to impose an enforced loan on the people of Jarra. Ali agreed, the cattle were driven off and other goods were seized and carried away. Shortly after this, Ali and his followers left Jarra, leaving the rebels and the people of Jarra to look after themselves. There was a real and pressing threat from Desse Kouliballi, who had already attacked Khasso and destroyed several towns while hunting down the rebels who had taken refuge there. It was thought likely that Desse Kouliballi would soon turn his attention to the Kaarta rebels in Ludamar, who now called on Ali to honour his side of the bargain and supply the two hundred cavalry they had hired. Ali procrastinated, then reneged on the agreement, telling the rebels that his cavalry were otherwise employed.

Mungo, whom Ali had allowed to remain in Jarra, now faced a

difficult decision. He had every reason to believe that if he remained in Ludamar he would either be killed, or held as a captive slave. If he could escape from Ludamar, he might be able to return to the Gambia with Johnson, or he could try and make his way to the east into Segu. However, if he went forward on his own, he faced great difficulties as he had no gold or trade goods wherewith to buy provisions, and without an interpreter he might have difficulty in making himself understood. Return to the Gambia and to England without accomplishing the object of his mission was unacceptable, so notwithstanding all the difficulties, he resolved to go forward if an opportunity to escape from Ludamar presented itself.

The rebels from Kaarta now presented Mungo with the opportunity to escape. They mounted a sortie into Kaarta with the intention of bringing the king's army to battle. Finding Desse Kouliballi's army much stronger than they had expected, they avoided combat and began plundering the towns and villages of the area. Desse Kouliballi needed no further excuse and marched his army towards Jarra, initiating a flight of the terrified population from the town. In the confusion and panic Mungo seized the opportunity to escape, mounted his horse and joined the refugees. On the road to the east he found Johnson and Daman Jumma also in flight from Jarra and joined up with them.

Mungo and his companions halted at the village of Queira, as he needed to rest his sick and emaciated horse. While they were there, Johnson saw Ali's chief slave and four other Moors arrive in the village and lodge with the *dooty*. Johnson also managed to discover that the Moors had come to seize Mungo and carry him to Ali at Bubaker. Johnson immediately warned Mungo, who made preparations to depart that night. Somewhat surprisingly the Moors made no attempt to take Mungo that evening, but retired for the night, after finding out where he slept. Towards dawn on 2 July Mungo said farewell to Johnson, and silently left the village on his horse. He had not gone far when three Moorish horsemen came chasing after him, brandishing their weapons. They quickly caught up with him and told him that he must return to Ali. Heartsick and in a state of numbed despair, Mungo accompanied them back towards the village. Suddenly, one of the Moors ordered him to untie the small bundle of clothes he was carrying and show them what was in it. Nothing interested them except his cloak, which one of them seized. Mungo pleaded for the return of the cloak, as it was of great use to him, protecting him from the rain by day and from mosquitoes by night. Two of the Moors rode off with the cloak and Mungo made as though to follow them, which the third Moor prevented him from doing. Suddenly he realised that they had not followed him to apprehend him, and take him back to Ali, but only to rob him. He thereupon turned his horse and rode off towards the east:

> It is impossible to describe the joy that arose in my mind when I looked around and concluded I was out of danger. I felt like one recovered from sickness; I breathed freer; I found unusual lightness in my limbs; even the Desert looked pleasant, and I dreaded nothing so much as falling in with some wandering parties of Moors, who might convey me back to the land of thieves and murderers from which I had just escaped.

7

To the Niger, and the return to Kamaila

Mungo was now on his way toward Segu but he was by no means out of danger. He was still in Ludamar, he had no resources for the purchase of food, his horse was in a wretched condition and he was in a desperate state himself, tormented by thirst and unable to find water in the wilderness. Towards evening on the day of his escape from the Moors at Queira he collapsed, thinking that he was about to die. He lost consciousness, but after a while recovered and resumed his journey. That night he suffered the experience of a sandstorm but to his great relief it was followed by a shower of rain. He spread his clean clothes on the ground and sucked the water from them. Travelling on by night he managed to avoid what was probably a Moorish encampment, and then attracted by the croaking of frogs — 'heavenly music to my ears' — he found some muddy pools, so full of puddocks that it was hard to see the water. Here he and his horse were able to quench their thirst. Mungo was by now very tired and very hungry, so notwithstanding the risks he entered a Foulah village, still within Ludamar, and sought aid from the *dooty*. This was denied him, so he begged for some food at a hut outside the village, receiving from an old woman a bowl of couscous from the previous evening's meal, and some corn for his horse. People gathered round while Mungo was feeding his horse, and it became apparent that some among them wished to seize him and take him back to Ali. Mungo reserved what was left of the corn, mounted his horse, and so as not to arouse suspicion that he was in flight from the Moors, headed back in a northerly direction, followed by all the children of the village, who trailed after him for a couple of miles. When none remained, he moved off into the woods to rest and get some sleep.

Later that day he awoke and resumed his march towards Segu. That night he slept by a pool in the woods but was much troubled by mosquitoes, and the presence nearby of wild animals, whose howling terrified his horse. At dawn he moved on and after some hours came to the camp of some Foulah shepherds, one of them inviting him to enter his tent and share his meal of corn and dates. The shepherd's wife and three children were in the tent, but when the shepherd mentioned that their guest was a Christian, a *'Nazarani'*, they began to cry, and fled outside and could not be persuaded to return. Mungo purchased some corn for his horse from the shepherd, though all he had for payment was a few brass buttons. Thanking the shepherd for his hospitality, Mungo left the camp and returned to the woods, where he again spent the night until awakened by the beasts he refers to as 'wolves'. During the following day, 5 July, he finally left Ludamar behind him and entered the kingdom of Segu, halting at the small town of Wawra, where he was hospitably received by the *dooty*. Here and throughout the Bambara kingdom of Segu Mungo aroused great curiosity wherever he went, but it was generally respectful and well meaning, except when Moors were present in some numbers.

Mungo was hospitably received at Dingyes, his next halting place, where his host, an elderly Foulah, begged Mungo to let him have a lock of his hair, wherewith to make a *saphie* (charm). The old man had been told that a *saphie* made from the hair of white men would give the possessor all the knowledge of the white men. Mungo complied with the request, realising that if this belief was widespread, he carried a valuable commodity on his head. The old Foulah cropped one side of Mungo's head pretty closely, and would have taken all Mungo's hair, if Mungo had not set his hat on his head, telling the old man that he wished to reserve some for another occasion.

Mungo was obliged to halt for four days at the small town of Wassiboo (Ouessebo), as the next stage of the journey was a long day's march through forest with no clear path, through which it was necessary to travel with a guide. Mungo stayed at the *dooty's* house and assisted members of his family in planting corn. On the fifth day, eight refugees from Kaarta

A Bambara man.

arrived in the town, having fled Ludamar rather than suffer under Ali's tyranny. They intended to travel to the capital and seek Mansong's permission to settle in Segu, and they offered to accompany Mungo on the trek through the forest. This they did, and more besides, for they stayed with him for several days, as they were travelling through stretches of country where lions were numerous. As they told Mungo, lions were much less likely to attack a party of people than a single individual. There were also places on the road where Moors sometimes ambushed travellers, and care was needed passing through them. The party was now travelling through attractive, fertile and well-watered country, where the refugees from Kaarta were minded to settle, if they could obtain the king's permission.

The reception Mungo and his companions received at the towns and villages where they halted for the night varied greatly, sometimes generously hospitable, sometimes grudging, while others refused to supply their needs, or in a few cases to receive them at all. On one occasion Mungo and his companions were taken for a party of Moors, and found the gates of the town closed against them, and the people under arms. It took a long time to convince the *dooty* and the people that they were not Moorish raiders and to obtain entry to the town. As the party neared Segu they found the area quite thickly populated, and they encountered many people on the road, going to, or coming from the city, including a coffle (a line of slaves linked together by cords or chains, or in some areas by wooden halters placed around the neck) of some seventy slaves, destined for what would probably be a death march for many of them, either to the salt workings in the Sahara desert or all the way to Morocco.

Mungo's horse was very weak, and from 13 July he could only ride it for a few miles each day, so was obliged to walk much of the way to Segu, driving the animal before him. Mungo's ragged appearance, his obvious poverty, his sick and exhausted horse, all seem to have been a source of some amusement in the towns and villages through which he passed some people taking him for a destitute Moor, returning from the pilgrimage to Mecca.

On 20 July Mungo was told that on the following day he would see the Niger, or Joliba, as it was called in the Bambara language. Mungo could not sleep for excitement and was waiting for the gates of the village to be opened, long before dawn. With the refugees from Kaarta, who had agreed to introduce Mungo to the king, he rode through some marshy ground to a point where one of his companions called out,

> *geo affili* (see the water), and looking forwards, I saw with infinite pleasure the great object of my mission — the long sought for majestic Niger, glittering in the morning sun, as broad as the Thames at Westminster, and flowing slowly *to the eastward*. I hastened to the brink, and, having drank of the water, lifted up my fervent thanks in prayer to the Great Ruler of all things, for having thus far crowned my endeavours with success.

Mungo was not surprised to discover that the river flowed to the east, though when he had left Britain he had been inclined to a contrary view, notwithstanding Major Houghton's report. However, during his journey he had repeatedly asked questions concerning the river and had invariably been told that the river's course was toward the rising sun.

Segu, the Bambara capital, a city of some 30,000 inhabitants according to Mungo's estimation, lay on both banks of the river in four separate walled quarters, the king residing on the further bank. Mungo noted that there were mosques in every quarter of the city, and that the ferry traffic across the river was well organised. The ferries, manned by the king's slaves, were long narrow canoes capable of carrying a good many people, horses and substantial loads. Since it was market day, a large crowd was waiting to cross over, and Mungo was worried by the presence of many Moors among them. Mungo waited for a ferry on the river bank for some two hours but was not allowed to cross. News of the arrival of the white man had reached Mansong, who sent over one of his officers to tell Mungo that he could not possibly see him until he knew what had brought him to Segu, and that he must not presume to cross the river without permission. Mungo was told to spend the night in a village some distance away, and that he would receive instructions as to how he should proceed on the following day. When Mungo reached the village, he was turned away from every door, the people regarding him with amazement and fear. He thought he might have to spend what promised to be a wild and stormy night out in the open; and moreover, it looked as though he might have to get what rest he could in the branches of a tree, from fear of lions and other wild animals. He had turned his horse loose and was preparing to ascend a tree, when a woman passing by and observing him asked after his situation. Mungo explained and with a compassionate look the woman picked up his saddle and bridle and invited Mungo to follow her to her hut. She spread a mat for him to sleep on, and finding that he was hungry obtained a fine fish, which she cooked for him. She invited him to take his rest and sleep, calling on her daughters, who had been staring at Mungo in astonishment since his entry into the hut, to resume their task of spinning cotton. This they did, accompanying the work with songs, one of them being about their guest, composed on the spot, and sung by one of the young women, the rest joining in a chorus:

The air was sweet and plaintive, and the words, literally translated, were these: "The winds roared and the rains fell. The poor white man, faint and weary, came and sat under our tree. He had no mother to bring him milk; no wife to grind his corn". Chorus "Let us pity the white man; no mother has he," etc., etc. Trifling as this recital may appear to the reader, to a person in my situation, the circumstance was affecting in the highest degree. I was oppressed by such unexpected kindness; and sleep fled from my eyes.

Mungo had nothing to give his landlady in the morning, except a couple of brass buttons, a very small token of his appreciation of her kindness. He found that the villagers had largely lost their fear of him, and he spent much of the day in conversation with them. He was concerned that he had heard nothing from the king, and learnt from the villagers that Mansong had received very unfavourable reports about him from the Moors and *slatees* resident in Segu. The following day a messenger arrived from Mansong to ask if Mungo had brought any presents. On learning that Mungo had been robbed of everything by the Moors and was destitute, the messenger returned to the king, telling Mungo to remain where he was. Later the same day, another messenger arrived to tell Mungo that the king's orders were that he must immediately leave the area of Segu. This messenger, who was appointed to guide Mungo to the town of Sansanding, also brought a bag containing 5,000 cowries, sent by Mansong to relieve Mungo's distress, and to enable him to buy provisions on the road. After some conversation with the guide, it became clear to Mungo that Mansong had ordered him to leave the vicinity of Segu, as he was concerned that he might not be able to protect Mungo from 'the blind and inveterate malice of the Moorish inhabitants'. The circumstances of Mungo's arrival in Segu, and the explanation he gave for his journey, may also have led Mansong to believe that Mungo was a spy, or that his journey had some secret purpose, and for that reason he would not receive him, or allow him to remain. The explanation that Mungo gave for his long and dangerous journey, namely that he had come to see the Joliba and follow its course, seemed implausible to many, including the guide appointed by Mansong, who asked Mungo if there were no rivers in his own country, and whether one river was not much like another! Mungo was sincerely grateful for Mansong's gift of cowries, which in that fertile land might keep him and his horse provisioned for the best part of two months. He would also discover and be grateful for the fact that as 'the king's stranger' he had protection, for he was not seriously molested or robbed during his entire stay in Segu.

Accompanied by the guide, Mungo left the area of Segu and headed toward the east. The guide was friendly and gave Mungo some account of Djenne and Timbuktu, and the country between them, this being Mungo's intended route. Though Djenne was nominally within the Bambara kingdom of Segu, it was largely controlled by the Moors, and Timbuktu was an independent Moorish kingdom. This news certainly gave Mungo food for thought, for he would again face the prospect 'of falling into the hands of men who would consider it not only justifiable, but meritorious, to destroy me'. However, having come so far, Mungo remained determined to continue his journey.

Passing through beautiful and well cultivated country, where the shea-nut tree grew in great abundance, the harvest of the nuts then being in progress, Mungo and the guide reached Sansanding, an important trading town of some 10,000 inhabitants, situated on the Niger. The black African inhabitants took Mungo to be a Moor, but it was not long before he was observed by Moors and his identity disclosed. He once again became the object of intense curiosity, several people claiming to have seen him before, one woman claiming to have worked for him in Senegal, others saying they had seen him on the Gold Coast. A crowd of Moors now assembled round him, with their usual arrogance and rudeness forcing the black Africans to stand at a distance. These Moors now questioned Mungo about his religion but finding that he did not speak Arabic, they sent for two men whom they said were Jews, apparently expecting that they would be able to converse with him. These Jews were compelled to conform to the religion of Islam, to the extent of joining in the public prayers, and it became apparent that the Moors expected Mungo to do the same, threatening to carry him to the mosque by force. Fortunately for Mungo, Counti Mamaadi the elderly *dooty*, intervened at this point, telling the crowd that as the stranger was under the king's protection, he could not allow him to be ill-treated, adding that the stranger would be sent on his way in the morning. However, the crowd insisted on taking Mungo to the door of the mosque and placing him on a high seat, so that he might be visible to the very large crowd that had gathered. The intrusive curiosity of the Moors persisted, even after the *dooty* had installed Mungo in a guest hut, as they climbed the surrounding compound walls and crowded into the court before the hut. Eventually, they left, whereupon Counti Mamaadi came to Mungo to request that he write a *saphie* for him, saying that while *saphies* made by Moors were good, those prepared by a white man must be better! Mungo obliged, and wrote out the Lord's Prayer for the good old man, whose timely intervention may have saved Mungo from serious ill-treatment, and possibly from death.

Mungo resumed his journey the following morning before the Moors could again assemble to harass him. The reception he received in the towns and villages where he stayed varied a good deal, with the *dooty* in one place treating Mungo and his guide hospitably, while in the next the *dooty* might refuse to receive him. The rains were now well set in, the rice fields and the swamps were under water and soon the Niger would flood. Travel by land was becoming increasingly difficult and would soon become impossible. Mosquitoes were everywhere, especially at night, and their bites made sleep impossible. Mungo's horse collapsed, and he was obliged to leave it in the care of one of his guides. He was in a bad way himself, feverish and very tired from lack of sleep. He arrived at the town of Silla, some seventy-five miles from Segu, on or about 29 July, and here he took the decision to turn back and head for the Gambia. He took the decision with reluctance but was forced to it by his ill health, exhaustion, hunger, and his very reasonable fear of the Moors, whose territory he was again about to enter if he continued toward Djenne and Timbuktu. He had nothing except a few cowries, and travel would soon become impossible, except by canoe.

Having taken the decision to return, Mungo made it his business to question the long-distance traders then in Silla, regarding the country to the east. He obtained useful information about the onward course of the river past Djenne, to Kabara — the port of Timbuktu, and toward Houssa (Hausa), though none of his informants could say where the river ended.

Mungo proposed to return on the south bank of the Niger but was told by the *dooty* that that would be impossible, on account of the rising water in the many creeks and swamps that lay on that side of the river. He was also told that the route along the north bank would soon become impassable, when the river overflowed its bank. On the second day after leaving Silla, Mungo was surprised to be reunited with his horse, now somewhat recovered, since he had not thought it would survive when he had left it with one of his guides. The journey along the north bank was a difficult one and at times he was leading his horse through water that reached his chest. The almost incessant rain also forced him to halt for several days in villages between Silla and Sansanding. As on the outward journey in some villages he was well received, in others poorly.

Mungo now realised that it was widely believed that he had entered the country as a spy, and that since Mansong had refused to see him, the headmen felt free to treat him as they pleased. Arriving in Sansanding, he found that the *dooty*, who had rescued him from the Moors of the town on the outward journey, did not seem pleased to see him return. However, late that evening the *dooty* came secretly to Mungo, to tell him that Mansong had sent people to follow him to Djenne, and bring him back. He also advised Mungo to move on quickly to the west, and to make no attempt to enter Segu, or any of its neighbouring villages. As if to confirm this warning, when Mungo arrived at the village of Kabra the following day, he was met at the gate by a man who would not allow him to enter, but conducted him round the walls, and urged him on towards the west. Mungo was now firmly convinced that Mansong, at the prompting of the Moors and *slatees*, had indeed sent out people to apprehend him. He made his way past Segu, and continued his journey to the west, travelling parallel to the river in the direction of Bamako.

His reception in the towns and villages along the way improved somewhat after he had left the immediate area of Segu, though he was never sure of shelter for the night nor of food for himself and his horse. On one occasion, arriving at a small village, the inhabitants refused him entry, though there were lions in the vicinity. Mungo remained close to the village, and during the evening became aware that a lion was prowling about close by. He pleaded with the villagers to let him in, but for some time they would not do so, taking Mungo to be a Moor. Finally, after Mungo had climbed a tree for safety, the *dooty* and his people opened the gate and let him in, convinced that he was not a Moor 'for no Moor ever waited any time at the gate of a village, without cursing the inhabitants'. Since the harvest had not yet been gathered in, food was in short supply in some places, and the people unwilling to sell. On several occasions, all Mungo could get was some raw corn, though in one large town he was able to get two good meals by writing *saphies* for a merchant and the *dooty*.

The country between Segu and Bamako was populous and fertile, but at this time of the year with the Niger in flood, much of it was under water. On several occasions Mungo and his horse were forced to swim across tributary streams. As he neared Bamako he observed that there were significant rapids on the Niger, and the force and roar of the water was very great. Arriving at Bamako on 23 August, Mungo was somewhat disappointed to find that it was quite a small town, though an important market for salt. Here Mungo sought and obtained information about the route to the west. He was told that the regular route was impassable at this time of year, on account of the rivers being in flood; but that a rough road through the hill country to the north west of Bamako remained open. Mungo set off next day, in the company of an itinerant musician who was supposed to show him the way. The musician took the wrong road and on realising his mistake abandoned Mungo, taking a path up the side of a hill that no horse could follow. Mungo retraced his steps and eventually found the right path up into the hills. From these hills he obtained a fine view of the country and in the far distance, away to the south-east, he observed some mountains, which he learnt were in the country of Kong. (This observation, though quite accurate, when received in Europe, had the unfortunate effect of lending confirmation to the belief that a great chain of mountains ran from Sierra Leone to the other side of the African continent.) Mungo spent the night in a remote walled village in a beautiful valley, where a Mandingo merchant and his family had taken refuge in a former war. Visitors rarely came to this secluded and fertile spot but Mungo was warmly welcomed and he and his horse were well looked after.

The next day, travelling through difficult hill country, Mungo was attacked and robbed by a group of Foulah brigands, who stole his horse, stripped him naked and took all his clothes, except for a ragged shirt, equally ragged trousers, his worn-out boots, and his hat, wherein he kept his notes. After the brigands had gone, Mungo came close to complete despair, as he records:

> I sat for some time looking around me with amazement and terror. Whichever way I turned, nothing appeared but danger and difficulty. I saw myself in the midst of a vast wilderness in the depth of the rainy season, naked and alone, surrounded by savage animals and men still more savage. I was five hundred miles from the nearest European settlement. All these circumstances crowded at once on my recollection; and I confess that my spirits began to fail me. I considered my fate as certain, and that I had no alternative, but to lie down and perish. The influence of religion, however, aided and supported me.

Mungo recalls in his book that at this point he observed a small but beautiful fruiting moss growing beside the place where he sat. The sight of such beauty, brought to its perfection by the hand of the Supreme Being, led him to reflect on his situation and to conclude that God, who had created man in His own image, would not desert him and that he should not give way to despair. Strengthened by such thoughts, he pulled himself together, and ignoring hunger and fatigue, he marched on to the Manding frontier town of Sibidooloo. Here he reported the robbery to the *mansa*, the chief of the town. The *mansa* was outraged to learn of Mungo's misfortune and swore that everything would be recovered and returned to him. He sent a messenger to inform the *dooty* at Bamako that the white man, who had lately been in that place, and who had enjoyed Mansong's protection, had been robbed by Foulah brigands, the subjects of the king of Fooladoo. Mungo gratefully accepted the *mansa's* invitation to remain with him until the messenger returned, but finding that a condition approaching famine prevailed in the town, and being unwilling to impose on the *mansa's* generosity, he sought permission to move on. The *mansa* agreed, but told him to go no further than the town of Wonda. Mungo journeyed on to Wonda, where he remained for ten days, much of that time sick with fever. Here, as elsewhere in Manding, there was a severe shortage of foodstuffs, and Mungo learnt that several poor women had sold children to the *mansa* in exchange for a supply of corn for themselves and the rest of their families.

On 6 September, eleven days after Mungo had been robbed, two men arrived from Sibidooloo, bringing his horse, his saddle and bridle, and his clothes. The following day Mungo's horse fell into a deep well, when the ground on which it was grazing gave way. The townspeople managed to get the horse out of the well, but the poor animal was in such a wretched condition, that Mungo decided to give the horse to the *mansa*, who might be able to take care of it, and restore it to health. Mungo sent his saddle and bridle to the *mansa* at Sibidooloo, this being the only return he could make for the trouble the *mansa* had gone to in recovering the stolen property.

Though still weak and feverish, Mungo decided to leave Wonda. Before he left, his hospitable landlord, the *mansa*, presented him with a spear and a bag for his few remaining clothes. Now on foot, Mungo journeyed on toward the west, travelling through hilly country. Despite the near famine conditions that prevailed in the area, he was generally well received and hospitably entertained in the towns and villages where he stayed, though in one town the *mansa* attempted to rob him, an attempt thwarted by Mungo's vigilance and the help of a townsman.

On 16 September, Mungo reached the small town of Kamaila, situated at the base of some rocky hills, where alluvial gold was collected in considerable quantity. Here he was taken to the house of one Karfa Taura, who was assembling a coffle of slaves to take to the Gambia when the rains were over. When Mungo arrived, Karfa Taura was reading aloud to several *slatees*, from an Arabic book. He inquired of Mungo, in a pleasant manner, whether he understood the Arabic. When Mungo answered in the negative, Karfa Taura sent someone to fetch a little book that had been brought from the west. This book was placed in Mungo's hands, and he was surprised and delighted to find that it was *The Book of Common Prayer*. Karfa expressed his pleasure on learning that Mungo could read the book, adding that he would be pleased to give him such assistance as was in his power. He told Mungo that further travel to the west, through the Jallonka wilderness, would be impossible for several months, and advised Mungo to remain with him in Kamaila, until the rains were over and the coffle was ready to depart. Mungo explained that he had no money and would have to press on, begging his way from place to place, or perish on the road. Karfa then offered Mungo accommodation, a plentiful supply of victuals and a safe conduct to the Gambia in return for whatever Mungo thought proper to give him on arrival there. Mungo suggested that the value of one slave might be appropriate and to this Karfa readily agreed, immediately ordering a hut to be prepared for him. Karfa was as good as his word and kept Mungo supplied with water, firewood and two good meals each day for the duration of his stay in Kamaila.

Within days of Mungo's arrival in Kamaila, already in a weak and feverish condition, his health deteriorated sharply. He collapsed with a raging fever, which remained with him for some five weeks, and he rarely left his hut. Towards the end of October, as the rains slackened off, and the country began to dry out, the fever finally left him. However, he was in a seriously debilitated state, so weak that he could hardly stand upright or walk without support. During November and December, with the onset of the dry season and cooler weather, his health rapidly improved and he gradually regained his strength. After he had recovered sufficiently, and having plenty of time, he recorded his impressions of the Mandingo people.

8

Mungo Park's observations on the Mandingo

Mungo Park devoted three chapters of his book to an account of the manners and customs of the Mandingo people, as he observed them in Kamaila and elsewhere in his travels. In modern ethnography, the term Mandingo is used to describe those who speak any one of a family of languages, collectively known as Mande. Most of the people Mungo Park refers to as Mandingo were probably from the group known today as the Malinke. However, other peoples of the area who speak a Mande language include the Bambara and Serahuli (Soninke). None of his observation relating to the Mandingo (Malinke) should be assumed to apply to other peoples he had encountered such as the Foulah and the Moors. Here space does not permit more than a selection of Mungo's more interesting observations on the Mandingo people and their culture.

Mungo's comments on the agricultural practices of the Mandingo are scattered around in his narrative but he does record most of the crops grown, and noted the absence of many of the tropical fruits found in the East and West Indies. He also noted that the cultivation of the soil was done with the hoe and records in one of his best descriptive passages the practice of burning off the grasslands during the dry season:

> a scene of terrific grandeur. In the middle of the night I could see the plains and mountains, as far as the eye could reach, variegated with lines of fire, and the light reflected in the sky made the heavens

appear in a blaze. In the day time pillars of smoke were seen in every direction; while the birds of prey were observed hovering round the conflagration, and pouncing down upon the snakes, lizards, and other reptiles, which attempted to escape from the flames. This annual burning is soon followed by a fresh and sweet verdure, and the country is thereby rendered more healthful and pleasant.

He described the Mandingo people as being 'a very gentle race; cheerful in their dispositions, inquisitive, credulous, simple and fond of flattery'. He did observe that while in general they did not steal from one another, they would readily steal from strangers, such as himself who had goods of value with them. However, he was quite prepared to acknowledge that strangers carrying valuable goods in Europe might well be robbed by the 'lower orders', the temptation being very great in both cases. Mungo contrasts what he saw as the pilfering disposition of the Mandingo with the disinterested charity shown towards him by so many people:

(Who)…(from the sovereign of Sego to the poor women who received me at different times into their cottages when I was perishing of hunger) sympathised with me in my sufferings, relieved my distresses, and contributed to my safety. This acknowledgement, however, is perhaps more particularly due to the female part of the nation. Among the men, as the reader must have seen, my reception, though generally kind, was sometimes otherwise. It varied according to the various tempers of those to whom I made application. The hardness of avarice in some, and the blindness of bigotry in others, had closed up the avenues to compassion; but I do not recollect a single instance of hardheartedness towards me in the women. In all my wanderings and wretchedness, I found them uniformly kind and compassionate…

Commenting on the filial affection and respect for the mother that he had observed in all the countries through which he travelled, Mungo records that the worst kinds of insult that could be offered to an African man were those that reflected on the character of his mother. He thought that the system of polygamy weakened the ties between father and child, since the father's interest was divided between the children of several

Sambou, griot Malinké à Niantanso.

A Malinke musician.

wives. This, he argued, had the effect of concentrating all of a mother's attention on the care and protection of her own offspring.

He outlined the customs of the Mandingo in the raising of children, and in rites of passage such as those associated with the naming of infants, circumcision, marriage and death. Custom appeared to give husbands great authority over wives, but Mungo saw relatively little evidence of cruelty towards wives by their husbands. However, he did observe that the Muslims in the community required their wives to be extremely submissive and deferential, and treated them more like hired servants than companions. He was of the opinion that most African husbands allowed their wives more freedom than did the jealous and suspicious Moors. He observed that while 'the Negro women are very cheerful and frank in their behaviour...', they were not inclined to intrigue and deception, and he thought that marital infidelity was uncommon.

Mungo gave some attention to the religious beliefs of the Mandingo. He was in no doubt as to their belief in a single God, and in reward and punishment in the afterlife. They did not pray to the Deity, except upon the appearance of the new moon, when they gave thanks to that Deity for the moon that had passed, and solicited his favour during the existence of the new moon. Otherwise, their view of the Creator was as a being so remote, and of so exalted a nature as to be indifferent to the supplications of mere mortals. In their view, the Creator entrusted the world to the care of a multitude of subordinate spirits, which were approachable through prayer and various ceremonies requiring sacrifice.

The general health of the Mandingo people received some attention from the young surgeon. He observed that few attained the age of sixty, and that most were old by the age of forty. Fevers and gastro-enteric disorders were common and often fatal. Mungo noted a sweating treatment for fever, which did bring relief to the patient. He also observed the addition of the bark of various trees to the food of those suffering from dysentery, though he thought these preparations were generally ineffective. Mungo was of the opinion that the Africans were better surgeons than physicians. Fractures and dislocations were successfully treated, abscesses were cauterised, cupping was employed on local inflammations, and effective dressings were compounded of leaves, shea-butter and other substances. He observed the presence of yaws, leprosy, elephantiasis, gonorrhoea and the Guinea worm in the Mandingo population.

Mungo paid some attention to the music and poetry of the Mandingo, taking note of several of their instruments, including the *korro*, an eighteen-stringed lyre, now more generally known as the *kora*, and the *balafou*, a type of xylophone. Among the musicians, there were professional praise-singers, sometimes itinerant and known as *jilli kea*, who composed extempore songs in honour of the chief men of the town or village, or any other person prepared to part with 'solid pudding for empty praise'. They also recited the great epic poems relating to Sundjata (Sundiata), the culture hero of the Mandingo nation. Others, generally itinerant, sang Islamic hymns, panegyrics in honour of the Prophet, and other forms of religious verse. Both groups were highly respected, and some among them became wealthy and influential..

In Mungo's opinion the Mandingo were an industrious people, a view contrary to that held by the European traders on the coast, who considered them indolent and inactive. They worked hard to produce what was needed for the subsistence of themselves and their families, but having few opportunities to profitably dispose of any surplus production, they only cultivated what ground was necessary for their own maintenance. Farming kept the people occupied during the rainy season and, in the dry season after the harvest the men turned to hunting, fishing, or perhaps some craft occupation, while the women spun cotton, wove and dyed cotton cloth. Mungo described the craft occupations of the Mandingo, observing that they recognised only two specialised crafts, tanning and leatherworking on one hand and iron smelting and blacksmith work on the other. Mungo had the opportunity, while at Kamaila, to observe the process by which iron was smelted by the Mandingo smiths, and he gives an excellent description of a craft that has now almost disappeared in Africa. As regards the other crafts, he wrote that almost anyone could learn how to weave, dye, sew, and make baskets and mats. While this was true, in practice there was a degree of specialisation in these crafts, though they might only be dry-season occupations for their practitioners.

Mungo extended his early impressions of the trade in slaves, and of African domestic slavery, in the notes he made while at Kamaila. He observed that three out of every four people in that part of Africa were slaves, and that those taken and sold to the European and American slave traders were, for the most part, already domestic slaves. The *slatees*, who brought slaves to the coast, preferred to deal in men, women and children who had been slaves from infancy. The *slatees* knew that those who had only known a condition of servitude were well accustomed to hunger and fatigue, and better able to withstand the hardships of a long and painful journey than free men, who were also more likely to try and escape. Free men who became slaves generally entered that condition as a result of capture in war, the most productive source of all slaves. There were other routes into slavery for free men, namely famine, insolvency and crime. During times of famine, men voluntarily surrendered their liberty in order to survive, while the parents of large families facing starvation might sell some of their children in order to preserve the rest of the family. Debtors, especially traders whose speculations miscarried, faced the prospect of being sold into slavery by their creditors if the sale of their property did not cover the value of the debt. The only crimes for which slavery was a possible punishment were murder, adultery and witchcraft, and Mungo thought that these offences were uncommon, or that other punishments were normally employed in such cases.

In his examination of the economy of the Mandingo, Mungo makes some observations on the obtaining of gold and on the trade in that commodity, and on the hunting of elephants and the trade in ivory. Though some alluvial gold was obtained by searching the beds of streams and washing the sand and gravel found there, more was obtained by mining. Mungo did not see the gold-bearing sand being dug from pits by men, but he did observe the women washing through the sand dug from these pits, so as to obtain the grains of gold dust that might be present. While some gold went to make ornaments for the women, most of it entered trade. Gold was a currency and was of special importance in trade for the rock salt brought from the desert by the Moors, or the sea salt brought by traders from the west. Gold also featured in the purchase of European goods brought from the coast by the *slatees*, and hence in their trade with the Europeans.

Elephants were present in great numbers in Kaarta, Segu and the hill country through which Mungo would pass on his journey to the Gambia, but everywhere they were hunted for their flesh, their hide and above all for their teeth, which were keenly sought by all the European traders. He describes in some detail the methods employed by the elephant hunters, generally four or five hunters working as a team, who might spend months during the dry season, roaming the country in search of their prey. Generally, the hunters sold the ivory to the *slatees*, who carried it to the coastal and riverside trading posts on asses, or on the heads of trade slaves.

Mungo concludes his observations on the economy of the Mandingo by noting that the products of agriculture — grains, tobacco, indigo, cotton, etc — did not feature in trade with the Europeans, and proceeds to some interesting and revealing reflections:

> the natives raise sufficient only for their own immediate expenditure; nor under the present system of their laws, manners, trade and

government, can anything further be expected from them. It cannot, however, admit of a doubt, that all the rich and valuable productions, both of the East and West Indies, might easily be naturalised and brought to the utmost perfection in the tropical parts of this immense continent. Nothing is wanting to this end but example, to enlighten the minds of the natives, and instruction, to enable them to direct their industry to proper objects. It was not possible for me to behold the wonderful fertility of the soil, the vast herds of cattle, proper both for labour and food, and a variety of other circumstances favourable to colonisation and agriculture — and reflect, withal, on the means which presented themselves of a vast inland navigation, without lamenting that a country so abundantly gifted and favoured by nature, should remain in its present savage and neglected state. Much more did I lament that a people of manners and a disposition so gentle and benevolent, should either be left as they are now, immersed in the gross and uncomfortable blindness of pagan superstition, or permitted to become converts to a system of bigotry and fanaticism, which, without enlightening the mind, often debases the heart.

In this passage we may observe the combined influences of Mungo Park's firm Christian convictions, and the belief in progress and improvement that lay at the heart of the Scottish Enlightenment. Mungo's argument pointed in the direction of Christian missionary involvement in Africa; and also towards some form of colonial intervention on the African continent, having as its aim the moral, social and economic improvement of the indigenous population, through education and example. So far as Africa was concerned, the agenda for the anti-slavery, liberal and humanitarian reform movements in Europe and America for the next half century was very largely shaped by debate around these themes and their practical implementation. Though these reform movements might have an influence on the development of European and American state policy towards Africa, this was seldom decisive, and they had very little influence on the commercial penetration of Africa.

With a slave coffle to the Gambia, and the return to Britain

In December 1796, Karfa Taura, Mungo Park's host, left Kamaila to go and buy slaves at the markets on the Niger. He left Mungo in the care of Fankooma, the local Muslim schoolmaster, a mild-mannered man. He was a strict adherent to the principles and practice of Islam, but was by no means intolerant towards those who differed from him. Fankooma had a number of Arabic books and manuscripts, and Mungo was surprised to discover that the Pentateuch, the Psalms of David and the Book of Isaiah were known to him, and to many other African converts to Islam. These Muslim converts were equally surprised to learn that Mungo was familiar with these books. As elsewhere in his travels, Mungo saw that Islam was rapidly extending its influence through the Koranic schools, such as the one maintained by Fankooma. Most of the children being taught at this school were the sons and daughters of pagans. Reflecting on this situation, Mungo deplored the fact that no serious effort was being made to spread Christianity to Africa, and went on to recommend that a simple introduction to the Christian faith be printed in Arabic and made available for distribution.

Karfa Taura returned to Kamaila with a young woman as his fourth wife and thirteen slaves, taken as prisoners of war by the Segu army. Mungo conversed with the slaves and learnt of the special horror with which Africans regarded sale to the European traders at the coast. The slaves knew that they would be taken beyond the sea. What they did not know was what awaited them across the ocean, and they firmly believed that they were being taken to be eaten by the white cannibals. They would not believe Mungo when he told them they would be employed in cultivation of the land. Since the fear of sale to the Europeans was so great, the *slatees* were compelled to keep the slaves in irons and keep a close watch on them lest they escape. Some few of the slaves bore their situation bravely, but most were sunk in a melancholy contemplation of their fate, torn from their homes and loved ones and facing an uncertain and forbidding future.

Mungo's few remaining clothes were so worn out that he felt ashamed to be seen in them, and he was sincerely grateful to Karfa for the gift of a shirt and trousers of the kind worn by Mandingo men. He was also grateful to Karfa for his continued support and his refusal to listen to those *slatees*, and three Moorish traders temporarily resident in Kamaila, who spread malicious stories about him and about Europeans in general. Subsequently it emerged that the three Moors, despite a pretence of piety, were thieving rogues, who had defrauded a merchant from the Fezzan of a substantial sum of money.

With the *slatees* and their slaves all assembled in Kamaila and its neighbourhood, the journey to the Gambia might have commenced during the month of February, but for one reason or another departure was repeatedly postponed. In 1796 the holy month of Ramadan fell between mid March and mid April, and a firm and final decision was taken to postpone departure until after the festival (*al-'id as-saghir*) that marked the end of the month of fasting. Mungo commented on the strict observance of the fast by the Muslims of Kamaila and their reverent and humble demeanour during Ramadan, in 'striking contrast to the savage intolerance and brutal bigotry which at this period characterise the Moors'. Finally the day of departure was fixed for 19 April, and on that day the caravan, or coffle, departed for the Gambia, with some ceremony. The coffle was made up of thirty-eight free people and domestic slaves, and thirty-five trade slaves, who while on the march were fastened to each other in groups of four, by a rope around the neck, and were put in irons during the night. Fankooma the schoolmaster and several of his students were among the free members of the party. He was returning to his home town of Malacotta, between the Senegal and Falemé rivers, after nine years' absence.

Parkia africana.
The locust bean tree.

The long march of some 500 miles in the hot season, much of it
through wild and rugged country, was exhausting, especially for some of
the trade slaves who from long confinement in irons were in poor
condition for a daily walk of twenty miles or more. Though the coffle
carried what might be called emergency rations for the journey, especially
that part of the route that lay through uninhabited country, there was an
expectation that they would be able to buy supplies along the way. Instead
in some areas they found villages where no grain was to be had at any
price, and the people were eating famine foods, including a paste extracted
from the pods of the locust bean tree, first brought to the attention of the
European botanists by Mungo Park, and named *Parkia africana.* (It was
Robert Brown, Mungo's near contemporary at the University of Edinburgh,
and one of the most outstanding botanists of the nineteenth century,
who proposed the name *Parkia africana* — now *Parkia biglobosa* — in Mungo
Park's honour).

One particularly distressing incident happened in the Jallonka wilderness during the early days of the march, when Nealee, one of Karfa Taura's female slaves, first refused food and then began to lag behind, complaining of great pain in her legs. Her load was taken from her and she was placed at the head of the column. At a rest halt the column was attacked by a huge swarm of bees after an attempt had been made to take the honey from their hive. Nealee was most severely stung and though she was given treatment, she refused to move another step, saying that she would rather die. She was whipped and after taking several blows she rose and walked on for some hours, when she attempted to run away. She was so weak that she quickly fell and the whip was again applied but to no effect. Karfa Taura ordered her to be placed on an ass but this proved impracticable as she could not sit erect and the ass was refractory. She was carried to that night's halting place in a kind of litter. The next day Nealee was so stiff and sore that she could neither walk nor stand and an attempt was made to tie her to the back of an ass, but Nealee could not, or would not, do anything to keep herself from falling off. The ass again proving recalcitrant, it was not long before Nealee was pitched to the ground, bruising herself badly:

Every attempt to carry her forward being thus found ineffectual, the general cry of the coffle was *kang-tegi, kang-tegi* (cut her throat, cut her throat), an operation I did not wish to see performed, and therefore marched onward with the foremost of the coffle. I had not walked above a mile, when one of Karfa's domestic slaves came up to me with poor Nealee's garment upon the end of his bow, and exclaimed, *Nealee affeeleeta* (Nealee is lost). I asked him whether the *slatees* had given him the garment as a reward for cutting her throat? He replied, that Karfa and the schoolmaster would not consent to that measure, but had left her on the road, where undoubtedly she soon perished, and was probably devoured by wild beasts.

This chilling incident made a great impression on the members of the coffle, especially those who were suffering from the pace and distances of the daily marches, and who feared that they might be the next to suffer the unfortunate woman's fate if they lagged behind or refused to go on. The march continued through the uninhabited wilderness without further

A slave coffle on the march.

incident, though evasive action was taken to avoid a raiding party thought to be in the area. Leaving the wilderness they entered villages where there was no food available for sale. In one of these villages, one of Fankooma's students was kidnapped by a villager. The boy was released when the kidnapper discovered that the schoolmaster came from Malacotta, only three days journey to the west. The abductor of the student no doubt realised that he could not keep the boy as a slave without the fact becoming widely known, and that for the same reason sale would be difficult.

The coffle crossed the Senegal river by a curious floating bridge, carried away each year by the river in flood, and rebuilt by the local people, who charged a small fee to all travellers who used it. Shortly after crossing the river, the *slatees* received news that a party of 200 of the Jallonka people had assembled near a town on their route in order to ambush and rob them. Evasive action was again taken but Karfa Taura was eventually obliged to hire guards to protect the coffle until it left the Jallonka country two days later.

Shortly before the coffle arrived in Malacotta, Fankooma was met by his brother in an emotional reunion. The coffle rested in the town for three days and its members were well entertained and supplied during their stay. On leaving Malacotta, they passed through another gold-producing area, where grains of the metal were found in white quartz. After Karfa Taura's coffle had crossed the Falemé river, they were joined by some Serahuli *slatees*, with a coffle of slaves they were taking to the Gambia. One of their slaves collapsed from weakness and exhaustion and was left behind with one of the Serahuli, the idea being that the slave would be rested and then brought on in the cool of the evening. That evening the Serahuli rejoined the party, without the exhausted slave, whom he said was dead. The general opinion was that the Serahuli had killed the slave, rather than be bothered with him, the Serahuli having a reputation for great cruelty in their treatment of slaves. Shortly after this incident, news was received that there was little demand for slaves on the Gambia, as no ships had arrived there for several months. On receiving this news the Serahuli *slatees* decided not to proceed to the Gambia, and left Karfa Taura's coffle, taking their slaves north towards Kajaaga.

On two occasions after crossing the Falemé river slaves from Karfa Taura's coffle were exchanged for slaves held by people in towns through which they passed. In one case an exhausted male slave was exchanged for a young woman, who had no idea of what was about to happen to her until the coffle was ready to leave the town:

> Never was a face of serenity more suddenly changed into a look of the deepest distress; the terror she manifested on having the load put upon her head, and the rope fastened round her neck, and the sorrow with which she bad adieu to her companions, were truly affecting.

On 31 May, Mungo again saw the Gambia river and on 4 June he reached Medina, where he had been hospitably received by the elderly king on his outward journey. Karfa Taura would not halt the coffle in Medina, but Mungo left a message for the king, who was dangerously ill, thanking him for his answered prayers for his safe return. At Mungo's suggestion the coffle was halted at Jindey until an opportunity to sell the slaves might arise. At this town, which was not far from Pisania, Karfa Taura rented some huts for the accommodation of the coffle, and a piece of land on which some crops could be grown for their maintenance.

Mungo, accompanied by Karfa Taura, left for Pisania on 9 June, but before leaving he bade farewell to his travelling companions, and in particular to the trade slaves:

> doomed, as I knew most of them to be, to a life of captivity and slavery in a foreign land....During a wearisome peregrination of more than five hundred British miles, exposed to the burning rays of the tropical sun, these poor slaves, amidst their own infinitely greater sufferings, would commiserate mine, and frequently of their own accord, bring water to quench my thirst, and at night collect branches and leaves to prepare me a bed in the wilderness. We parted with reciprocal expressions of regret and benediction. My good wishes and prayers were all I could bestow upon them, and it afforded me some consolation to be told, that they were sensible I had no more to give.

On arriving at Tendacunda, Mungo and his companions were hospitably received at the house of the Seniora Camilla, an elderly African woman who spoke English and had met Mungo before he left the Gambia. His appearance was so altered that at first she took him to be a Moor, and was greatly astonished to discover his identity. She told him that he had long since been given up for dead, information having been received that he had been murdered by the Moors of Ludamar. Mungo asked if there was any news of Johnson and Demba, and learnt that neither had returned.

Dr Laidley had moved his trading post to Kayee (Kaiai), a few miles down river from Pisania, but Robert Ainsley was still there, and on learning that Mungo was with Seniora Camilla, rode over and invited him to stay at Pisania until Dr Laidley returned from a short business trip down river. Dr Laidley returned on 12 June and greeted Mungo 'with great joy and satisfaction, as one risen from the dead'. He undertook to honour all Mungo's obligations against a draft upon the African Association, and promised to assist Karfa Taura in disposing of his slaves to the best advantage, whenever a ship should arrive. Mungo doubled the amount he had promised Karfa Taura in Kamaila, the previous September, and arranged for a generous present to be sent to Fankooma, at Malacotta.

As no ship was expected and the rainy season was setting in, Mungo suggested that Karfa Taura should return to his people at Jindey, and on

14 June they parted. Mungo thought they would meet again before he would be able to leave, as ships were not generally expected on the Gambia at that time of year. However, the following day the American ship *Charlestown* arrived on the river, and since the traders had many slaves to sell, they quickly agreed to purchase the ship's entire cargo of rum and tobacco, and deliver slaves to the value of that cargo. These transactions were completed in two days, and on 17 June Mungo boarded the *Charlestown* at Kayee, bidding farewell to Dr Laidley and his other friends on the river. Though he faced a long and circuitous journey, this was to be preferred to waiting through the rainy season on the Gambia for a ship returning directly to Britain. The journey down the river was tedious and unhealthy, five crewmen and three slaves dying of fever before the ship reached the sea. The *Charlestown's* master took the ship to the French island of Gorée, just to the south of Cape Verde, to complete his cargo of slaves, but was unable to leave there for want of provisions until early October. As the ship's surgeon was one of those who had died of fever in the Gambia, Mungo acted as surgeon, not that he was able to do much to relieve the dreadful sufferings of the slaves on the voyage across the Atlantic. Mungo was critical of the American method of confining and securing slaves on board ship, comparing it unfavourably with that in use in British ships. (From 1788, following the passage of the Dolben Act by the British Parliament, the number of slaves a British slave ship could carry had been limited according to the size of the ship. This measure, which was later strengthened, probably had some effect in limiting slave mortality in British slave ships.)

The *Charlestown* was not in good condition, indeed she was scarcely seaworthy; she leaked so badly that three weeks out from Gorée the pumps were being manned around the clock, and some of the fitter slaves had to be released from their fetters to labour at the pumps. The crew were afraid that the ship would sink, as the pumps made no impression on the slowly rising water, and they forced the captain to make for the West Indies rather than South Carolina. The *Charlestown* just made it into St John's, Antigua, though she was nearly wrecked when she struck a rock in the approaches to the island. The ship was condemned as unfit for sea, and the surviving slaves, many in a weak and emaciated condition, were sold in Antigua. The total number of slaves received by the *Charlestown* was 130, and of these at least twenty died between departure from Kayee and arrival in Antigua, a rate of mortality of around fifteen per cent, a fairly high figure for the late eighteenth century, probably accounted for by the long delay at Gorée.

Mungo cashed a draft on Sir Joseph Banks, and obtained passage for England in the *Chesterfield Packet*, leaving Antigua on 24 November and arriving in Falmouth on 22 December. He arrived in London early in the morning of Christmas Day and apparently bumped into James Dickson, his brother-in-law, in the gardens of the British Museum, the care of these being Dickson's responsibility. Though such a meeting at such a time and place probably came as a considerable surprise to both of them, Dickson certainly knew that Mungo was alive and on his way home. In October 1797, Sir Joseph Banks had received a letter from Mungo, together with a statement of his account with Dr Laidley. Sir Joseph passed on the good news to Major Rennell, who informed James Dickson and through him the Park family in Scotland.

England and Scotland, 1798–1803

Shortly after his return Mungo Park called on Sir Joseph Banks, who was delighted to see him, eager to receive a first-hand account of his travels and discoveries, and proud of the fact that, through the young Scotsman's endeavours, the African Association had achieved a resounding success. Sir Joseph made sure that publicity was given to Mungo's journey into the far interior of West Africa through short articles in the newspapers. Mungo briefly became something of a social celebrity, but fashionable London society was not for him. His reserved demeanour was not well received by those who hosted receptions, and the bored socialites who attended them and looked for entertainment from the traveller were disappointed in him.

Sir Joseph Banks made it clear to Mungo that a written report of his travels would be required for presentation to the African Association's annual meeting in May. Mungo really needed time for rest and recovery, but he could not leave London for Scotland until the report was written. He had little experience of writing, and it became apparent that he would not have the report ready in time without professional assistance. The geographical side of the report, involving detailed analysis of the information Mungo had collected, and the production of a map, was placed in the hands of Major Rennell, whom Mungo already knew. For the narrative of the journey, Mungo was introduced to Bryan Edwards, MP, Secretary to the African Association in succession to Henry Beaufoy.

Edwards had made a fortune in the West Indies, and was a leading opponent of the Parliamentary campaign for the abolition of the slave trade, led by William Wilberforce, MP. Edwards was also an experienced author, who had written several pamphlets, and *A History of the British Colonies in the West Indies,* published in two volumes in London in 1793. Using material supplied by Mungo, he worked quickly and soon had a summary narrative ready for approval by Park and Banks. This summary, with the title *Abstract from the Travels into the Interior of Africa* together with Major Rennell's *Geographical Illustrations of Mr. Park's Journey,* was printed for private circulation to members of the African Association, who met towards the end of May 1798. This meeting unanimously passed a resolution expressing the Association's 'warmest approbation' for Mungo Park's endeavours in carrying out the objectives of the mission he had undertaken.

Mungo left London for Scotland in early June to be reunited with his family. Only Mungo's mother and his unmarried brother John, who now held the tenancy of the farm, remained at Foulshiels. No doubt the whole family, with the possible exception of the Dicksons from London, were all assembled to welcome home the traveller, now well known, even famous. Once the celebrations were over Mungo settled down to the work of writing a full account of his travels. The African Association continued to pay him while he was working on the book, and had also agreed to his keeping whatever profits might result from the sale of the completed work. Since Mungo was not a practised writer, it was agreed that he should send drafts of the work to Bryan Edwards for editing and stylistic improvement. The work went slowly at first, but as Mungo gained confidence he found an appropriate style and as Edwards observed when writing to Sir Joseph Banks in late January 1799 'he improves in his style so much by practice that his journal now requires but little correction, and some parts he has lately sent to me, are equal to anything in the English language'. The book, *Travels in the Interior Districts of Africa, Performed in the Years 1795, 1796 and 1797,* which also contained Major Rennell's *Geographical Illustrations of Africa,* was published by George Nicol in London in April 1799. The book was an instant success, with two more editions that year and another in 1800. A French translation appeared in 1799, with a German translation and an American edition in 1800.

While working on the book in 1798–9, Mungo would break off from time to time to take walks in the countryside he knew and loved, or would visit friends in Selkirk. No doubt he visited his old master Dr Thomas Anderson, renewed his longstanding friendship with the doctor's son Alexander, and would again have met the doctor's daughter Allison, now an attractive young woman of eighteen. Soon Mungo was paying court to Allison, he proposed marriage, was accepted, and they agreed to wed in 1799.

In September 1798 a certain coolness developed in the relationship between Mungo Park and Sir Joseph Banks, over a proposal that Sir Joseph had put to Mungo in May. The proposal was for Mungo to go to Australia to undertake exploration in the interior on behalf of the British Government. In May, Mungo had accepted the idea, though he told Sir Joseph that he thought the proposed remuneration was inadequate. Taking note of Mungo's objection, Sir Joseph Banks advised the Under-Secretary of State that Mungo would accept the appointment to Australia for a daily remuneration of 12s 6d. When Sir Joseph Banks and Mungo had discussed the matter in May 1798, Sir Joseph had led Mungo to believe that he could secure an improved offer from the Government, once the African Association had commended Park for his work in West Africa, which it duly did.

When Mungo saw the Under-Secretary of State in September 1798, he found that the Government was not prepared to offer more than 10s 0d a day, the letter from Sir Joseph Banks having been overlooked or misplaced. Mungo told the Under-Secretary of State that 10s 0d a day, with no provision for an outfit and equipment, was less than what he had been led to expect, and he refused the appointment. When Sir Joseph learnt of Mungo's refusal, he persuaded the authorities to improve their offer, and he personally undertook to provide the funds for an outfit and equipment. It was too late; Mungo's pride was involved, and nothing Sir Joseph could do or say would induce him to reconsider his decision. During the month of September an increasingly severe and formal correspondence passed between Mungo and Sir Joseph Banks, with the latter also writing apologetically to the Under-Secretary, referring to Mungo as 'this fickle Scotsman'. While these exchanges were taking place, Sir Joseph received a letter from his old friend, and Mungo's brother-in-law James Dickson, in which he refers to his having been told by his wife, Mungo's elder sister 'that their [sic] is some private connection, a love affair in Scotland'. Sir Joseph now knew that Mungo had a reason for refusing the appointment that he had not revealed and he tried to get him to admit to it, but with no success. Sir Joseph then wrote to the Under-Secretary to inform him that he was convinced that Mungo's refusal to accept the improved offer was to be attributed to undisclosed motives:

> I am more and more convinced daily that his refusal is owing to an Intention he has newly formed of settling himself here: if so he is totally useless to us. Had his enthusiasm continued he would have made an excellent Instrument in the hands of a good Director. As that is gone he is no longer worth a Farthing.

There may have been at least one other factor that influenced Mungo in his decision to refuse the appointment to Australia. The original plan was for him to leave in September 1798, or shortly after, together with Philip Gidley King, the newly appointed Governor of the penal colony of New South Wales. When Mungo came to London in September 1798, he had written no more than one third of *Travels in the Interior Districts of Africa,* and an early departure for Australia would have meant the indefinite postponement of publication. If the book proved to be a success it might be expected to yield a significant return, an important consideration for a young man contemplating marriage.

Sir Joseph's disappointment and irritation with Mungo, perhaps exacerbated by an attack of gout, did not last long, and their relationship did not suffer in the longer term as a result of these misunderstandings, bureaucratic shortcomings and Mungo's reticence regarding his personal plans. Sir Joseph soon found a replacement for Mungo in his plans for Australian exploration in the botanist Robert Brown from Montrose, who did important scientific work in Australia on the *Investigator* expedition of 1801–3, commanded by Lieutenant Matthew Flinders.

With the appearance of Mungo Park's *Travels* in the spring of 1799, Sir Joseph Banks took the opportunity presented by the Annual Meeting of the African Association on 25 May to praise Mungo for the courage, patience and judgement he had shown during his travels, and to congratulate him, Bryan Edwards and Major Rennell on the book. He went on to urge the British Government to build on Mungo's achievements by sending a well-armed military force to the region to establish a British presence on the Niger, with a secure line of communication back to the sea. Sir Joseph spoke of commercial opportunities, the presence of gold and the need to take action to prevent rival European nations from gaining the upper hand in the region. The African Association, responding to Sir Joseph's prompting, then adopted a resolution requiring its Committee to again urge the Government to appoint a Consul for the Senegambia region and dispatch a force 'to take possession of the Banks of the Joliba, and explore the Interior from thence'. With the passing of this resolution the African Association took several steps towards advocating an imperial strategy for Britain in West Africa, lobbying for the use of military force to secure commercial opportunities, and to forestall any ambitions the French might have for control of the Senegambia region. These imperial intentions are underlined in the letter Sir Joseph Banks wrote to Lord Liverpool, President of the Board of Trade, in June 1799, when he presented a memorandum, based on the African Association's resolution, for consideration by the Cabinet:

> Should the undertaking be fully resolved upon the first step of Government must be to secure to the British throne, either by Conquest or by Treaty the whole of the Coast of Africa from Arguin to Sierra Leone; or at least to procure the cession of the River Senegal, as that River will always afford an easy passage to any rival nation who means to molest the Countries on the banks of the Joliba...

Sir Joseph's letter advances reasons for the adoption of this policy with what can only be described as an imperialist agenda — the desire for commercial gain, fear of the ambitions of a European rival, a sense of moral superiority over the peoples of the region, and the idea of a civilising mission.

Mungo's book appeared at a time when the debate in Britain between those who supported slavery and the slave trade, and those that argued for the abolition of the slave trade and opposed the institution of slavery, had entered a critical phase. Mungo had seen the slave trade and African domestic slavery at first hand, and had written about both, especially the latter. What he did not do was come down firmly for or against the slave trade and slavery. This led to a curious situation, with Abolitionists using his material on the horrors of the slave trade, while those who opposed abolition referred to the absence of any condemnation of the slave trade, or of slavery, in his book. Mungo was very well aware that domestic slavery was firmly embedded in African society and at the end of his chapter on slavery in Mandingo society, he deliberately avoided making any statement as to how far African domestic slavery was sustained by the Atlantic slave trade, writing that it was 'neither within my province, nor in my power, to explain'. He went on to observe that in his opinion the ending of the slave trade would have relatively little effect on African domestic slavery, suggesting that such effects as it did have might not be as 'beneficial, as many wise and worthy persons fondly expect'. This cautious, and one might add, realistic observation was Mungo's only known public statement of opinion regarding the slave trade or slavery; though members of his family consistently maintained that in private conversation he had always expressed a great abhorrence of slavery and the slave trade. No one who reads Mungo's book can doubt but that he was deeply sympathetic to the sufferings of the slaves he met, particularly those with whom he travelled from Kamaila to the Gambia. It is probable that he was in principle opposed to the slave trade but was reluctant to speak out against it, partly because any statement from him against the trade would split the African Association, whose employee he was until 25 May 1799, and perhaps because he felt constrained from making statements on matters of public policy, at least at that time. In this context some attention deserves to be given to the political background in Britain, Europe and the Caribbean in the period leading up to the appearance of Mungo's *Travels*.

While the cause of anti-slavery had been gaining ground in Britain in the period 1788–92, the international crisis that followed in the wake of the French Revolution had all but stopped the British anti-slavery movement in its tracks. Constitutional reformers in Britain, including many of those involved in campaigns against the slave trade, were branded as Jacobins and dangerous revolutionaries. The French Revolution had spread to the French possessions in the Caribbean, with a major slave revolt taking place in St Domingue (Haiti) in 1791, this being followed by British intervention on the Royalist and slave-owning side in the French Caribbean in 1793. The British Government's aim was acquisition of the French islands, and the crushing of the slave revolt in St Domingue. Martinique, Guadeloupe and St Lucia were occupied by British troops.

Parts of revolutionary St Domingue were also occupied, and war waged by the British against both the French Republican forces and the former slaves in St Domingue, led by Toussaint-l'Ouverture. French Republican forces recaptured Guadeloupe and St Lucia in 1794. Major slave revolts occurred in the British Caribbean islands of St Vincent and Grenada in 1795, with a Maroon rebellion in Jamaica in the same year. The British recaptured St Lucia after a hard and bitter struggle in 1796–7, and the revolts in St Vincent and Grenada were suppressed over the same period, though in both St Lucia and St Vincent the British commanders found it necessary to offer terms to at least some of their opponents in order to bring the fighting to an end. These wars in the Lesser Antilles, known to the British press as 'The Brigand Wars', cost the British some 40,000 casualties, with a further 20,000 casualties in St Domingue, before they decided to withdraw from that island in 1798.

These campaigns achieved very little for Britain in terms of imperial gains and cost a great deal both in terms of blood and treasure, with an estimated £16–20 million spent on campaigns in the West Indies between 1793–8. While these losses and the failure to achieve anything of importance in that theatre of war led to Parliamentary questioning of British war aims and imperial policy generally, both the domestic and international situations were correctly perceived as dangerous and threatening by the oligarchy that ruled Hanoverian Britain. The war with revolutionary France was going badly; French successes on the battlefield in Europe had left Britain virtually isolated and facing the prospect of invasion. Early in 1797 there was a serious financial crisis, and in the spring of that year seamen of the Royal Navy mutinied at Spithead and the Nore. In Ireland the armed revolt of the United Irishmen in 1798, which had received French support, was followed by a savage repression. The Treason and Sedition Act of 1795 and other measures were employed to stamp out anything that smacked of Republicanism and opposition to the established order.

In the 1790s in Britain something close to a 'white terror', orchestrated by the Government, was in operation, with civil liberties suspended and spies and informers everywhere. With the connivance of magistrates, 'Church & King' mobs attacked and destroyed the property of radicals and dissenters. Show trials of moderate reformers accused of sedition were held; in Scotland such trials taking place with hand-picked juries, and judges obedient to the will of Henry Dundas, virtual dictator of Scotland from 1783–1806.

Even if Mungo Park had been minded to write a critical denunciation of the Atlantic slave trade, or to speak out against slavery in all or any of its forms, the times were not propitious. While there is no evidence to suggest that he had any intention of writing such a book, or publicly declaiming against the slave trade and slavery, we can be sure that if he had such intentions, he would have been strongly advised against doing so by Sir Joseph Banks and others. In 1798–9, when Mungo was writing the book, he had some expectation of future service in the employment of the British Government, if not in Australia, then perhaps at some future date in the Senegambia. Sir Joseph Banks had led the African Association to propose to Government that it adopt a forward policy in that area, and it seems clear that Sir Joseph was prepared to recommend Mungo for a role in any expedition that the Government might send there. If Mungo had hopes of future Government employment, it would not have been in his interest to risk being branded as an opponent of the established order, a dangerous radical, a friend to rebellious slaves, by the powerful West India lobby in Parliament and their friends in Government.

With the successful appearance of *Travels...*, Mungo returned to Scotland to make preparations for his marriage to Allison Anderson, which took place in Selkirk on 2 August 1799. Mungo's 'lovely Allie' was a tall and attractive young woman, described as being 'amiable in disposition, with no special mental endowments, and if anything somewhat frivolous and pleasure loving'. Mungo, who at the time of his marriage was close to his twenty-eighth birthday, was around six foot tall, and the portraits painted of him at this time show a handsome, fine-featured, wavy-haired and blue-eyed young man. However, his African experiences had affected his health physically, and perhaps mentally as well. For several years he was afflicted with what some biographers have described as dyspepsia or indigestion, though the description given by Gibbon does suggest something rather more serious 'racked with pains that would send him raving across his bed or across a chair biting twisted lips'. He also suffered terrible nightmares, apparently reliving his experiences as Ali's captive in Ludamar. In 1804 Mungo told Walter Scott that he had left out of the book material that 'related solely to his own personal adventures and escapes', and it has been generally assumed by Mungo's biographers that these omissions relate to some serious ill-treatment that he experienced at Benowm or Bubaker.

Mungo had made some money from *Travels in the Interior Districts of Africa* but it was far from being a fortune. He needed to occupy himself, if for no other reason than that he was now a married man and would soon have a family to support, for Alison was pregnant and a son, named Mungo after his grandfather and father, was born towards the end of May 1800. Mungo is believed to have declined an offer of employment in the West Indies, said to have been made to him by Bryan Edwards some time before his death in July 1800. Mungo certainly discussed employment prospects when he met Sir Joseph Banks in London early in 1800. Mungo would have known of the steps Sir Joseph had taken to persuade the Government to send out an expedition to establish a British presence on the Niger, and had good reason to expect to be called upon to participate in such an expedition, once a decision had been taken to proceed. Sir Joseph probably told Mungo that there was little immediate prospect of an expedition to the Niger receiving government approval, and other employment possibilities were discussed. Nothing came of these discussions with Sir Joseph Banks and others whom Mungo may have approached in London early in 1800. However, his thoughts continued to run on the idea of another expedition to the Niger, for when he learnt that the island of Gorée had been captured from the French in April 1800, he wrote to Sir Joseph suggesting that the time was ripe for a new expedition to the Niger, and offered his services to Government, without result.

As the year advanced, with no call for his services forthcoming from the British Government, Mungo began to consider resuming his profession. Early in 1801 he travelled to London to take an examination that qualified him as a Member of the Royal College of Surgeons of London, formed from the Company of Surgeons, from whom he had obtained his Licence as an Assistant Surgeon with the East India Company back in 1793. He clearly had no great wish to resume the practice of his profession, for he continued to cast about for alternatives, giving consideration to the idea of emigration to New South Wales; and negotiating with Charles William Henry Scott, Earl of Dalkeith, heir to the Duke of Buccleuch and Queensberry, for the tenancy of a farm. When Mungo and Sir Joseph Banks met in London early in 1801, Sir Joseph discouraged him from proceeding with the idea of emigration to Australia, still a penal colony with very few free settlers, and largely controlled by a clique of brutal and avaricious officers from the New South Wales Corps, probably the most disreputable regiment ever created by the Crown. The idea of taking on the tenancy of a farm was also dropped, perhaps because of the high rent required and the high price of livestock at the time, factors that 'made it rather a dangerous speculation' as Mungo wrote to Sir Joseph in October 1801.

In September 1801, Allison had given birth to their second child, a daughter Elizabeth; around the same time Mungo entered into partnership negotiations with Dr James Reid, an elderly surgeon, and at that time Provost of the small market town of Peebles, in the valley of the Tweed some twenty miles from Selkirk by road. Mungo rejected the terms proposed for the partnership, but decided to set up in Peebles on his own account. In early October 1801 Mungo, Allison and the two children moved to Peebles, taking lodgings with a Mr Oman, a retired schoolmaster. Later the family moved into a small house in the Northgate. Mungo also rented premises in the nearby High Street to serve as a surgery and dispensary. These premises still existed in the 1860s and were described by William Chambers as a 'miserable den', where Mungo experienced 'some of the difficulties incidental to the life of a country surgeon'.

Mungo resumed his profession with much reluctance and certainly hoped for early action from the Government in respect of the African Association's long standing proposals for another expedition to the Niger. If the call should come, as he wrote to Sir Joseph Banks, he would resign his position to his brother Adam, who had qualified in 1798, or to his brother-in-law Alexander, adding:

> In the meantime I hope my friends will not relax in their endeavours to serve me. A country surgeon is at best a laborious occupation; and I will gladly hang up the lancet and the plaister ladle whenever I can obtain a more eligible situation.

The practice of medicine in a Scottish market town, serving a large area of scattered villages, hamlets, isolated farms and cottages, was onerous and poorly rewarded. Throughout the first quarter of the nineteenth century, there is known to have been great poverty in Peebles and the

A young Walter Scott.
Drawing by
J E Henning, c1806.

surrounding district, and this would have had consequences for Mungo Park as a medical practitioner, in terms of a heavy workload and an uncertain income.

Mungo spoke to Walter Scott about his experiences, and his feelings concerning the life and work of a country doctor, when the two became friends for a few short months in 1804, and Scott drew on them when he came to write *The Surgeon's Daughter*. Here Scott wrote of the hard life of a country doctor:

he is day and night at the service of every one who may command his assistance within a circle of forty miles in diameter, untraversed by roads in many directions, and including moors, mountains, rivers and lakes. For late and dangerous journeys through an inaccessible country for services of the most essential kind, rendered at the expense, or risk at least, of his own health and life, the Scottish village doctor receives at best a very moderate recompense, often one which is totally inadequate, and very frequently none whatsoever....I have heard the celebrated traveller Mungo Park, who had experienced both courses of life, rather give the preference to travelling as a discoverer in Africa, than to wandering, by night and day, the wilds of his native land in the capacity of a country medical practitioner....But his was not the heart which grudged the labour that relieved human misery. In short, there is no creature in Scotland that works harder and is more poorly requited than the country doctor, unless, perhaps it may be his horse. (*Chronicles of the Canongate*, 1827)

Notwithstanding Mungo's distaste for the work of a country doctor, the available evidence suggests that he was a conscientious and compassionate physician, whose work was highly thought of locally, and who was known to give his services free to the poor of the district.

Mungo had several friends in Peebles and its neighbourhood, among them Dr Adam Fergusson, author of *An Essay on the History of Civil Society* (1767), and former Professor of Moral Philosophy at the University of Edinburgh, who lived in retirement at Hallyards in the Manor Valley, not far from Peebles. Mungo frequently visited Dr Fergusson, and at Hallyards he is known to have met other scholars, including Dugald Stewart, who had succeeded Fergusson in the Chair of Moral Philosophy at Edinburgh. Mungo was also welcome in the homes of some of the local gentry, notably Sir John Hay, and had several friends among the townsfolk, including Colonel John Murray, Alexander Wilkinson the town clerk, and James Chambers, father of the brothers William and Robert Chambers, founders of the famous Edinburgh publishing house.

Following the resumption of war with France in 1803, and with it the threat of an invasion by Napoleon's army, volunteer home defence forces were created all over the British Isles. Mungo joined the Tweeddale Yeomanry, a volunteer cavalry force, commanded by Sir James Montgomery. Many of the Yeomanry units created during the Napoleonic Wars adopted striking uniforms, and the Tweeddale Yeomanry Cavalry were no exception, wearing white breeches, blue jackets with yellow collars and silver lace trim, and bearskin helmets with white hackles, but it is not known if Mungo ever wore this uniform.

However, Mungo did write a staunchly patriotic song for the Tweeddale Cavalry, singing it himself to the tune of '*Willie was a wanton wag*' at one of their social occasions. This was thought to be the only surviving example of Mungo's poetry, but a marginal manuscript note in the British Library copy of *The Life of Mungo Park* (Edinburgh, 1835) by H B, refers to his 'Sleep on My Sweet Babie' in Ross's *Collection of Scottish Songs*. I reproduce this poem here, since it appears to have been overlooked by other biographers:

Sleep on My Sweet Babie.
Written by Mr Mungo Park with Symphonies & Accompanyments.
Sleep on my sweet Babie, may nothing distress thee,
May sorrow like mine be a stranger to thee
Thy father no more shall with rapture caress thee,
No more will behold his sweet Babie and me.
Soft, soft be thy rest, thou companion of sorrow,
The morning of life it looks gloomy on thee,
Thy father is fallen in the Lowlands of Holland,
He sleeps far remote from his Babie and me.

Thy father is fallen, our stay and protector,
And with thee my Babie, ah! where shall I flee,
The World, I fear, will sadly neglect us,
They feel not the wants of my Babie and me,
Dear image of him, who has left us for ever,
Thou last beam of comfort allotted to me,
Through clouds of distress, shine forth on thy mother,
And cheer with a smile, her who lives only for thee.

The poem was set to music by John Ross, born in Newcastle-upon-Tyne, but for many years organist at St Paul's, Aberdeen, who composed or arranged the music for a large number of Scottish songs. Mungo's poem and the score are to be found in *A Select Collection of Ancient and Modern Scottish Airs, adapted for the Voice, with Introductory and Concluding Symphonies and Accompaniments for the Piano Forte composed by John Ross,*

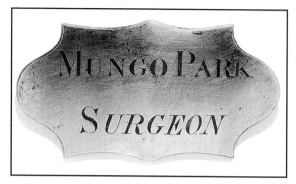

Brass plate from Mungo Park's surgery in Peebles, where he was in practice from October 1801 to May 1804. Now on display in the Museum of Scotland, Edinburgh.

Organist, St Paul's, Aberdeen. Printed and Sold by John Hamilton, 24 North Bridge Street, Edinburgh. The British Library copy of this work carries no date, though the catalogue gives the date 1803.

The reference in the text to the death of the infant's father in the Lowlands of Holland gives a possible clue to the occasion for the poem's composition. On 11 October 1797 the British North Sea Fleet, under the command of Admiral Adam Duncan, comprehensively defeated a Dutch Fleet, under the command of Admiral Jan de Winter, off Camperdown, on the coast of Holland. In late August 1799, a British military force, under the command of General Sir Ralph Abercromby, staged an invasion of North Holland, occupying an area north of Amsterdam until the end of November. This is not the place to comment on the campaign of 1799, except to observe that British casualties were heavy in a series of battles and skirmishes with Dutch and French troops. It may be noted that five Scottish regiments, including the Scots Guards, 1st Regiment of Foot (Royal Scots) and the 25th Regiment of Foot (King's Own Scottish Borderers) were involved in the North Holland campaign, and that the 1st and 25th Regiments of Foot were traditionally recruited from the Lothians and the Scottish Border Counties. Mungo's poem may have been a lament for the widow and child of someone he knew who had been killed, or had died from wounds or other causes in the North Holland campaign, or at Camperdown; or more generally as a lament for all the widows and children of those who died in these actions.

Background to the second expedition, 1803–5

Throughout the period 1801–3 Mungo was hoping for, and indeed expecting to receive, a call from the British Government for service in West Africa. Finally, in September 1803 it came in a cryptic letter from Sir Joseph Banks, requiring his immediate presence in London to see Lord Hobart, Secretary of State for War and the Colonies, for the purpose of discussing his role in an expedition that the Government had under consideration.

The idea of a Government-sponsored expedition to trace the further course of the Niger probably came about as the result of Sir Joseph Bank's lobbying. In 1802 he had alerted the British Government to proposals made in France for the adoption of a vigorous imperial policy on the West African coast. If adopted and executed, these proposals would have meant France taking control of the entire coast from the Senegal River to Cape Palmas (Liberia); proposals that echoed but went somewhat further than those recommended to the British Government by Sir Joseph Banks in 1799, and which clearly threatened British interests in the Gambia and Sierra Leone. Sir Joseph recommended, among other things, that a British military presence be re-established on James Island, some twenty-five miles up the Gambia river, the fort there having been abandoned following its destruction by the French in 1779. He also recommended that trading posts be established and free-trade treaties be made with local chiefs as far inland as the Falemé river. Discussions took place within Government, and several West African 'experts' were called on to advise. Plans for an expedition were drawn up in 1802, but nothing came of them at that time. However, in July 1803 the British Government did approve plans to raise a military force for an expedition to West Africa, with the objective of reducing and then occupying St Louis and the surrounding area, the sole remaining French possession in the region, at the mouth of the Senegal river. The summoning of Mungo Park to London in September 1803 was probably connected with plans for this expedition, and was likely to have been the result of further lobbying by Sir Joseph Banks, once he knew that action to forestall possible French moves in West Africa had been authorised. Sir Joseph was likely to have suggested that the opportunity be taken to continue the exploration of the Niger, and would have told Ministers that it was highly probable that Mungo Park would be available to lead such an expedition.

The plan put to Mungo in 1803 appears to have been to send him out to the Senegambia in company with the military expedition. Mungo would have no part in military operations against the French, but he would have an escort of twenty-five soldiers for an expedition to the Niger to discover its termination. Where the idea of a military escort came from is not clear, but Mungo does not appear to have raised any objection, though he knew that caravans in Africa did not proceed in this way. While trading caravans would be armed for protection against chance attack by bandits, the invariable method of securing safe passage through an area was by means of payments to local rulers, and might involve the hiring of local men to serve as escorts when passing through dangerous country.

Mungo was ready to accept the terms offered, 10s 0d per day subsistence and £200 for each year spent in Africa, but before finally committing himself he went back to Scotland to consult Allison, who in March 1803 had given birth to Thomas, their second son. Allison is said to have raised no objection to his leaving for this expedition, though there is some doubt about this. Allison, by this time, would have realised that Mungo was driven by an ambition to complete the mission he had been forced to abandon at Silla in 1796. She would have known of Mungo's dissatisfaction with the life of a country doctor, and she probably realised that he could not settle into family life and the practice of his profession, or anything else, until he had again made an attempt to solve the mystery of the Niger.

Mungo finally took the decision to accept the appointment offered to him by Lord Hobart after consulting Sir Joseph Banks, who of course urged him to accept. While Mungo waited for a summons to London, Alexander Anderson, his brother-in-law and friend since schooldays, volunteered to join the expedition. Late in December 1803 Mungo travelled to London, only to learn that the plans for the expedition had been significantly altered. Mungo was now to take charge of a party of 200 soldiers, who were apparently already on their way to West Africa, the task being to open a trade route from the Gambia to the Niger, with no encouragement being given to the idea of following the course of that river to its termination. Mungo obtained permission for Alexander Anderson to join the expedition on the same terms as his own. He also secured Government approval for a pension to be paid to Allison and the family in the event of his death.

Though Mungo may not have known it, the plans for his expedition were linked to a much more ambitious scheme for a large military expedition whose object would be to take control of the gold trade, and involved the capture and occupation of Timbuktu. What Mungo might have thought of such a hare-brained scheme, if it was ever put to him, is not known. However, the author of the plan, a certain Colonel Charles Stevenson, did have a couple of excellent ideas. For health reasons, he insisted that all long marches should take place during the dry season; and he also recommended that black soldiers from the West Indies be employed in these West African operations.

Between January and March 1804 there appears to have been a great deal of chopping and changing of plans for the expedition, together with much uncertainty as to whether it would take place at all during what remained of the dry season of 1803–4. Further complications would have arisen when news was received that on 18 January 1804, a superior French force, coming from the colony of Cayenne in South America, had taken Gorée, at that time garrisoned by soldiers of the Royal African Corps. Gorée was retaken by the Royal Navy on 7 March 1804, and again garrisoned by the Royal African Corps. At some point during the period January to March 1804 it would have become clear to the Secretary of State, and to Mungo, that there was no possibility of the expedition setting out from Britain before September 1804, at the earliest. Mungo returned to Scotland in March, taking with him Sidi Ombark Bouby, a Moroccan whom he had engaged to teach him Arabic, and who probably created as much of a sensation in Peebles and Selkirk as ever Mungo had done in Ludamar or Segu. Omback the Moor, as he was familiarly referred to in Peebles, seems to have been well thought of in the locality, and he apparently enjoyed his stay with the Park family in Scotland.

During March 1804 the plans for the expedition were again revised, and scaled down. The new plan was for Mungo to lead a party of 150 soldiers to the Niger, in the dry season of 1804–5, negotiating his passage and avoiding conflict with the local inhabitants. Colonel Stevenson would follow with a larger contingent and would be instructed not to use force, unless his men encountered the French, or were attacked. This plan was never implemented, no doubt because of the change in Government that took place in May 1804, with the resignation of Henry Addington and the King's appointment of William Pitt to succeed him as Prime Minister. Pitt appointed his friend Lord Camden as Secretary of State for War and the Colonies. Lord Camden had significantly different ideas to those of his predecessor regarding West Africa. His main policy objective seems to have been the elimination of the French presence on the Senegal river, so as to prevent its use as a base for privateers bent on harassing British trade. So far as Lord Camden was concerned, Mungo Park's exploratory mission to the Niger could go ahead without direct reference to the military expedition against the French position in Senegal, except in one vitally important respect — transport. Mungo Park and Alexander Anderson, with supplies for their expedition, would have to travel out to West Africa with troops or supplies for the naval and military expedition against the French, which would be launched from Gorée.

Mungo closed his surgery in Peebles in May 1804, and moved with his family and Sidi Ombark Bouby to Foulshiels, while waiting for further news from London. Shortly after the move to the old family home, Mungo's elder brother Archibald introduced him to Walter Scott, the Shirra (Sheriff) of Selkirkshire, then starting to make his name as a poet, and who at that time resided at Ashiestiel in the Tweed Valley, a three to four mile ride from Foulshiels, over the ridge between the Broomy Law and the Three Brethren. The two shared an interest in the ballads and legends of the Borders, Mungo giving Scott some verses for *The Sang of the Outlaw Murray* that he had not previously heard, and possibly other material. A friendship quickly developed and Mungo was able to relax in Walter Scott's company, talking freely about his experiences in Africa, something he rarely did except with his closest friends. Early in their friendship, Scott realised that Mungo was consumed with a determination to return to Africa. Their final parting, which has something of the stuff of legend about it, took place in September 1804, high up on the ridge overlooking the valleys of the Tweed and Yarrow. Mungo's horse stumbled and nearly fell as they approached the point where Mungo would leave and Walter Scott would return to Ashiestiel. Scott said to Mungo; 'I am afraid, Mungo, that is a bad omen'. Mungo replied, quoting from the old ballad *Edom o' Gordon*, 'Freits [omens] follow those who look to them', smiled at his friend, and rode away.

In September 1804 Mungo received the call to attend on Lord Camden in London, and with it came the moment that Mungo and Allison, who was six months pregnant with their fourth child, must have dreaded. There are several accounts of their final parting, and it is difficult to say which is the authentic one. One of these accounts suggests that Mungo could not bear to say a proper goodbye to his wife and children, and misled Allison by telling her he was going to Edinburgh on business and would return, when he had no intention of doing so. In another account of their parting, from a woman who had been a maidservant in the Park household at the time, Mungo told Allison that he would stay if she asked him not to go; this she would not do, and said to him 'Go, and do your duty'.

Mungo seems to have thought that there was a possibility of cancellation of all plans for an expedition to the Niger when he left Scotland for London. When he was received by Lord Camden on 26 September, he was told that Government had dropped the idea of a large military expedition to the interior, but did intend to proceed with an attack on the French in Senegal and a mission of discovery and investigation into the interior, that Mungo Park was invited to lead. Lord Camden asked Mungo for a written statement of his ideas for the expedition, and called upon Sir Joseph Banks to take on the overall direction of the enterprise. Lord Camden also told Sir Joseph that he hoped it would be possible for Mungo to leave for West Africa by the middle of October. Mungo drew up a plan, presumably in consultation with Sir Joseph, and submitted it to Lord Camden on 4 October.

Mungo's plan for the expedition, which he may have worked on while in Scotland over the summer, had as its principal objectives: 'the extension of British Commerce and the enlargement of our Geographical Knowledge'. He would gather intelligence relating to trade and trade routes, with particular reference to the future development of a secure route by means of which British merchandise might be transported from the Gambia to the Niger. The vegetable and mineral products, the manufactures, the forms of government and of society in the countries through which the expedition passed would also be studied. The possibilities for British colonisation of areas within those countries would also be examined.

Mungo proposed taking thirty-five European soldiers from the Royal African Corps garrison at Gorée, six carpenters to build two boats for the proposed voyage on the Niger, and fifteen to twenty Africans from Gorée, mainly artisans. He supplied a detailed list of his requirements, which included fifty asses, six horses or mules, clothing, tools, arms, trade goods for supplies and presents, etc. Mungo proposed to sail to the Cape Verde Islands, where he would buy the livestock, then proceed to Gorée for volunteers from the garrison and the African community on the island, and from there sail to the Gambia. The expedition would march from the Gambia through Bondu, Kajaaga, Khasso and Fooladoo to Segu, where he would seek the friendship and protection of Mansong, while building a boat for a voyage down the Niger to Djenne, Kabara, Houssa (Hausa), Nyffe (Nupe), Kashna (Katsina) and Wangara.

This list of places that the expedition might visit reflected Major James Rennell's interpretation of the information that Mungo had brought back from his first expedition, supplemented by material from two other travellers, Friedrich K Hornemann and William G Browne. Hornemann, a young German, had been recruited by the African Association to try and penetrate through to West Africa from the North. He travelled to Cairo in 1797, before Mungo Park's return, and succeeded in joining a caravan bound for Murzuk in the Fezzan. From Tripoli and Murzuk he sent back useful reports on the Fezzan and parts of the Sahara, together with information he had obtained about Borno and Haussa, including the fact that Haussa was not an Empire, but a group of independent states that included Katsina and Kano. Nothing more was ever heard from Hornemann, though news was received in 1805 that he had been in Katsina. Much later it was learnt that he had travelled on towards the south and had died, probably at a town in Nupe, only a short distance north of the Niger. Browne, an independent traveller, in 1792–3 had travelled south from Cairo to Darfur, where he had been detained by the ruler until 1796. Browne had gleaned information about rivers that flowed to the north and west, and of a lake, that lay to the south-west of Darfur.

Among the mysteries of West Africa for the European geographers was the location of the country of Wangara. Major Rennell believed it to be a district in Borno, where the Niger emptied itself into a great lake or morass. What no one in Europe then realised was that Wangara, or Wangarawa, is the name of a people, an African trading diaspora of Mande origins, that is to say a people who trace their origins back to the far west, to parts of the Senegambia and Upper Niger regions. Wangara and Wangarawa were to be found in many parts of West Africa, including the Bariba and Hausa states. For example, there were at least two places with the name Wangarawa in the state of Katsina, and a thriving community of Wangarawa merchants were long settled in Katsina city itself. Since the names Wangara and Wangarawa referred to a scattered trading community, whose name sometimes came to be applied to places where they had settled, it is hardly surprising that it created some confusion for the European geographers. The name appeared to move around the map, shifting in relation to places whose location they thought they knew, from a position to the south-west of Timbuktu, to a position south of Katsina, to a position in Borno.

In Europe in the early 1800s there were four theories about the termination of the Niger. Following Mungo Park's first expedition, there was general agreement that it flowed from the west toward the east. What remained in dispute was the direction the Niger took after passing Kabara and Timbuktu. All the theories suggested that it flowed on toward the east for a considerable distance, through the countries named in Mungo Park's plan. The theory favoured by Major Rennell was that the Niger emptied itself into a lake or morass in Borno, roughly in the position of Lake Chad. Others still held to the view that the Niger eventually joined the Nile of Egypt, and referred to information gathered by Hornemann that apparently supported that theory. The two remaining theories suggested that after flowing to the east, the Niger either turned due south, or to the south and west. The first of these alternatives was advanced by one George Maxwell, a trader on the west coast of Africa, who had spent some time around the mouth of the Congo, a very large river with no known source. Maxwell had written to Mungo Park in July 1804, suggesting that the Niger might find its outlet to the sea as the Congo, supporting his suggestion by reference to the timing of the flood on both rivers. Mungo enthusiastically adopted this theory, and in so doing accepted the prospect of a voyage of not less than 3,000 miles, through totally unknown country. The remaining theory was advanced by Christian Gottleib Reichard, a German academic geographer, who in articles published in German geographic journals in 1802 and 1803, suggested that the Niger, after flowing for a great distance toward the east, then turned south and west, eventually discharging its waters into the Bights of Benin and Biafra, through a vast delta. If Major Rennell and Sir Joseph Banks had known of Reichard's theory in 1804, as they could have done; they certainly would have rejected it, largely because of their continued belief in the existence of the Mountains of Kong, which were assumed to stretch right across West Africa, blocking the outflow of the Niger into the Atlantic. Indeed Major Rennell explicitly rejected Reichard's theory, in letters to Sir Joseph Banks, after that theory was referred to by James Wishaw in the 1815 edition of Mungo Park's *Journal of a Mission to the Interior of Africa in the Year 1805*.

Lord Camden was pleased with Mungo Park's plan for the expedition but decided to send him to see Major Rennell before giving it formal approval. Major Rennell had doubts about the commercial possibilities of West Africa that had excited both Lord Camden and Sir Joseph Banks. He also held firmly to his belief that the Niger terminated in a lake or morass in Borno, and dismissed the Congo theory. Rennell felt that the planned expedition was altogether too dangerous an undertaking, and apparently succeeded in persuading Mungo to reconsider his decision to accept Lord Camden's offer. However, any doubts that Mungo may have had following his meeting with Rennell soon disappeared; for when he reported to Lord Camden that Rennell had serious misgivings about the expedition, he told him that he remained firmly resolved to proceed with the venture. Sir Joseph Banks supported Mungo's decision, while acknowledging that the risks that he would have to face were very great.

Plans for the naval and military expedition against the French in Senegal had received the King's approval in early October 1804, but had to be revised when news was received that the French at St Louis were in greater strength than had been supposed and were well prepared to receive an attack. More troops were required for the expedition but at that time none could be spared, with Spain on the point of joining France in the war against Britain and her allies. Consequently, the military expedition to Senegal was again postponed, a decision that was to have the most serious consequences for the expedition to the Niger, which might well have been cancelled at this point had not Lord Camden remained keen for it to go ahead.

Mungo may have hoped that it would not take long to find transport for West Africa but in this he was to be disappointed. Lord Camden's office may have done its best but nothing was available until the end of the year, when passage was arranged on the transport *Crescent*. Mungo must have become increasingly concerned about the delay, since it meant the loss of two to three months of the best time in which to travel in West Africa. It would appear that he made the Secretary of State aware of his anxieties, and of his horror of the rainy season, especially as a time for travelling. In mid December Lord Camden sought the advice of Sir Joseph Banks as to whether or not the expedition should proceed. Banks recommended that it should go ahead, estimating that if the expedition got away before 8 January 1805, Mungo and his party would reach the Niger in early June. This was a very tight timetable that made no allowance for delays or unforeseen difficulties and Mungo would have known it.

Mungo was kept busy during November and December organising supplies for the expedition, meeting shipping agents and no doubt trying hard to move things along at the War and Colonial Office. In December, Mungo would have heard from Scotland that Allison had given birth to Archibald, the son he never saw, on the sixteenth of the month. Also around this time another volunteer for the expedition came forward from Selkirk. George Scott, the twenty-five year old son of a tenant farmer, was a talented draughtsman who was seeking adventure, and no doubt an opportunity to make his name as an artist in foreign parts. Mungo recommended George Scott to the Colonial Office as draughtsman to the expedition, and the appointment was approved.

On 31 December 1804 Lord Camden wrote to the Admiralty, at the King's command, requiring the Navy to provide an escort for the transport *Crescent*, the ship assigned to carry Mungo Park from Portsmouth to West Africa. Two days later Lord Camden, wrote to Mungo giving him formal instructions for his mission. The aims of the expedition were to be the further exploration of the Niger and the gathering of commercially useful intelligence. Mungo Park and Alexander Anderson were granted temporary military commissions as Captain and Lieutenant respectively. Mungo was advised that he could recruit up to forty-five men from the garrison at Gorée. He was also told that he could engage such African labour as he needed, if necessary 'by purchase', and could freely choose the route he would follow from the Niger, should it be necessary to leave the river in the interior.

A later letter from Lord Camden's office laid out the financial terms offered to Mungo for the support of his family during his absence, and for a payment of £3,000 for the support of Allison and the family, in the event of his death on the expedition. Alexander Anderson was unmarried, but if he were to die on the expedition, his father would receive a payment of £1,000. If nothing was heard from them for two and a half years from the date of departure, they were to be assumed dead and the payments made.

The departure of the expedition continued to be delayed until well into January. Mungo Park, Alexander Anderson and George Scott did not leave London for Portsmouth until 22 January. In Portsmouth, Mungo collected four carpenters, who were to build a boat when the expedition reached the Niger. These carpenters were probably tradesmen who had been 'pressed' into the navy, navy defaulters or men sentenced to transportation. More delays for a variety of reasons prevented the departure of the *Crescent* until the early morning of 31 January, when she sailed together with the escorting sloop *Eugenie*.

12

The Second Expedition to the Niger

Mungo Park must have been greatly relieved when the *Crescent* and *Eugenie* finally stood out into the English Channel, but at the same time he ought to have been worried. Three months of the best travelling weather had been lost, and while it was still just possible for the expedition to reach the Niger before the heavy rains began, any further delays or accidents would rapidly reduce their chances of success.

The plan for the expedition required a visit to the Portuguese colony of the Cape Verde Islands for the purpose of buying livestock. This voyage usually took three weeks but contrary winds, the taking of evasive action to avoid possible French privateers, and the fact that the *Crescent* and *Eugenie* were both slow sailers, meant that five weeks passed before the two ships dropped anchor off Porto Praya on the island of St Jago on 8 March. Here Mungo entered into negotiations with the avaricious Governor, who used his position to extort a high price for the asses, and clapped two men into jail for selling below that price. Mungo also purchased fodder for the asses but on finding that short measure was being given, he protested to the Governor, who had the measure checked and on finding it short had little choice but to adjust the price in Mungo's favour. Mungo took the twenty dollars he had saved and placing them on the Governor's table asked him, in the presence of witnesses, to arrange for the distribution of that sum to the poor. General surprise greeted Mungo's gesture but he had made his point.

It took several days to get the asses and the fodder loaded aboard the *Crescent* and the expedition did not leave Porto Praya until 20 March. Strong and contrary winds and currents delayed the two ships on the 450-mile voyage to Gorée, which they did not reach until 28 March. During the stormy voyage two asses died, while others were injured.

Major Richard Lloyd, the commander of the Royal African Corps garrison at Gorée, welcomed the expedition and dealt with Mungo Park's requirements with efficiency and dispatch. The strength of the garrison was somewhat depleted through sickness, but Major Lloyd was able to spare thirty-five men, and an officer — Lieutenant John Martyn, who was quick to volunteer for service with the expedition. When volunteers were called for from the ranks on 29 March, most of the garrison came forward, perhaps induced by the promise of double pay, and a free discharge from the service if their conduct was reported to have been good. The volunteers may also have sought escape from the tedium of garrison duty, and may have looked forward to the prospect of some adventure and perhaps some action. Mungo Park was pleased that Lieutenant Martyn had volunteered, since he knew the men and together with other officers from the garrison, could assist him in making a selection. Mungo needed men who were physically fit, and if possible with some manual skill. The possession of useful skills became a serious requirement, when it became clear that none of the African artisans resident on Gorée were prepared to volunteer for the expedition. Two sailors from HMS *Squirrel*, which had put into Gorée to make some repairs to damaged masts, also volunteered for the expedition and were accepted, on the promise of double pay and freedom from impressment in the future.

The Royal African Corps was not one of the *élite* units of the British Army, indeed it appears to have consisted very largely of men that other regiments and corps did not want. However, the record suggests that the soldiers of the Corps acquitted themselves well in action, and on Mungo Park's expedition discipline did not break down, even when things were at their worst. Many of those who joined the Corps were men who had faced a flogging for breaches of discipline in other units. They might be offered the Royal African Corps as an alternative, one which many would have chosen, since a flogging in the army could mean serious injury, permanent disablement or even death. Service at the British forts along the West African coast from Gorée in Senegal to Whydah on the Slave

Coast was regarded throughout the British Army as a punishment and for many unfortunate men it was tantamount to a death sentence. Garrison service on the West African coast was not conducive to physical fitness and good health, as Mungo Park would soon discover.

The *Crescent,* with the members of the expedition on board, sailed from Gorée on 6 April, in company with the *Eugenie,* arriving at the port of Jillifree on the Gambia river on the following day. Here the sloop parted company, while the *Crescent* continued on up-river, reaching Kayee on 15 April. The expedition disembarked at Kayee, and began making preparations for departure, unloading equipment and organising the loads for the asses. More asses had to be purchased from local traders to replace those that had died, or had been seriously injured on the voyage from Porto Praya.

Mungo's search for Africans who would be willing to accompany the expedition at least as far as the Niger remained unsuccessful until he met Isaaco, a Sarahuli trader, resident in the Gambia, who was prepared to accompany the expedition to the Niger, for the price of two slaves, approximately £40. Isaaco made the journey with his wife and at least one child, and an unspecified number of attendants, probably domestic slaves.

Before departing from Kayee on 27 April, Mungo wrote a dispatch on the progress of the expedition for Lord Camden, and sent letters to Allison, Sir Joseph Banks, James Dickson and Dr Thomas Anderson, his father-in-law, to whom he consigned the will he had made. Though Mungo's letters express nothing but a confident optimism, it would have been astonishing if he had not been secretly worried. He was now well behind Sir Joseph Banks' very tight timetable and had perhaps six weeks in which to reach the Niger, over 500 miles away, before the heavy rains set in. This was not an impossible target for a small party of fit and experienced men, travelling light, but Mungo's caravan did not answer to that description. The asses Mungo had purchased at St Jago seem to have been difficult to manage, may not have been used to carrying loads, and do not appear to have been well suited to the environment on the mainland. It is doubtful whether many of Mungo's men were experienced ass-drivers, and as events were to demonstrate they were neither fit nor in good health. The caravan was relatively large, and the packs carried by the asses were large, heavy and difficult to load.

Did Mungo ever consider halting the expedition and waiting out the wet season, either at Gorée, or in the Gambia? The answer is that he probably did not the die was cast on the day he left England. He knew then that time was short, but he also knew that if he urged Lord Camden to postpone the expedition for eight months, the plans for the expedition might again be changed or cancelled altogether. In January 1805, it may have appeared to Mungo that there remained a narrow window of opportunity for a successful expedition, and that this opportunity might never occur again, at least not for him. If Mungo had halted the expedition at Gorée, or on the Gambia, he might well have been recalled, and even if that had not happened the soldiers might have been required for other duties. Mungo would have known that an expedition was planned for the expulsion of the French from Senegal. If that went ahead while he was at Gorée, or on the Gambia, his volunteers would probably have been required for some part in those operations.

The expedition left Kayee on 27 April, and marched to Pisania, where it remained for one week while attempts were made to sort out various problems and more asses were purchased. Leaving Pisania on 4 May, it took the expedition one week to reach Medina, a distance Mungo had covered in three days on his first expedition. Progress was slow, partly on account of the extreme heat at that time of the year, which meant that the men and animals were rested during the heat of the day, and partly, perhaps, because of a lack of decisive leadership. A whole day was wasted in a dispute over payment for access to wells, and an evening march was cancelled because of the alleged presence of bandits in some woods through which the expedition would have to pass.

Isaaco had warned Mungo that news of a heavily laden caravan, ripe for plundering, had preceded the expedition. This advance information had whetted the appetites of minor chiefs and headmen, as Isaaco and Mungo were to discover when they reached a village in the kingdom of Wuli, where the headman was accustomed to extorting extra tributes from passing caravans. Isaaco had been sent ahead to talk to this headman, who decided to take him hostage, then had him flogged, and put one of his attendants in irons. Mungo seems to have been quite nonplussed by this high-handed treatment of Isaaco. He consulted with Anderson and Martyn, but decided not to risk a night attack on the village for the purpose of releasing the hostages, lest innocent people be killed. However, the decision was taken to attack in the morning if Isaaco and his man were not released. Early next morning they were released, though the headman had kept Isaaco's gun and sword. The headman continued to demand a tribute and eventually settled with Mungo for one third of his original demand.

On 26 May a near disaster occurred as the caravan was making camp for the night. While some asses were being unloaded, they and their drivers were attacked by a swarm of bees. In the resulting panic a cooking fire got out of control and threatened to destroy all the expedition's baggage. Fortunately, the loads were saved, for if a significant amount had been lost, the expedition could not have continued. Though none of the men were seriously injured, six asses were lost, or died from bee stings.

At the village of Badoo, two days later, the caravan met a slave coffle headed for the Gambia, and Mungo took the opportunity to write letters to Allison and to Sir Joseph Banks. Both letters were misleading, for he wrote that they were half way to the Niger, which they expected to reach by 27 June. In fact they had only covered one third of the distance, and with the rains expected very soon, there was no possibility of the expedition reaching the Niger by that date.

Some days later the caravan encountered a local chief who threatened to ensure that the caravan was attacked and plundered in the forest if he did not receive a large addition to the customary presents. This chief, who had a reputation for avarice, demanded more with every addition that Mungo made to the spoils, until Mungo finally lost patience and called the chief's bluff by refusing to give anything more. The chief, pleased with his haul, allowed the caravan to proceed unmolested.

In early June the rains commenced in earnest, and with the rains a time of trial and dreadful suffering began for the expedition. Within a week of the beginning of the rains nearly all the members of the expedition were suffering from malaria, or dysentery, or a sickness whose precise nature is not known but which might have been jaundice. On 10 June Mungo recorded in his posthumously published journal, the start of the horrors that accompanied them for the rest of their journey to the Niger:

The tornado which took place on our arrival (at the halting place for the night), had an instant effect on the health of the soldiers, and proved to us to be the beginning of sorrow. I had proudly flattered myself that we should reach the Niger with a very moderate loss;…But now the rain had set in, and I trembled to think that we were only half way through our journey. The rain had not commenced three minutes before many of the soldiers were affected with vomiting, others fell asleep, and seemed as if half intoxicated. I felt a strong inclination to sleep during the storm; and as soon as it was over I fell asleep on the wet ground, although I used every exertion to keep myself awake. The soldiers likewise fell asleep on the wet bundles.

By 12 June twelve of the soldiers were sick but the caravan struggled on. With the benefit of hindsight it can be argued that the expedition should have halted at that point to look after the sick, who with rest and such limited treatment as it was possible to give, might have recovered, though with fever and dysentery there was always a risk of recurrence. The exposure of the sick to the rigours of a march forward to the Niger, or back toward the Gambia, was fraught with risks, not only for the sick but for the caravan as a whole. Mungo, who could have drawn upon his own experience of sickness in 1795 and 1796, never seems to have given thought to the possibility of halting the caravan. There were certainly risks in halting and staying where they were, but there were grave risks in all the options that lay before him. The fateful decision that now placed the caravan in deep trouble had been taken in London in December 1804, by Lord Camden acting on the advice of Sir Joseph Banks. Regrettably, Mungo Park also shares in the responsibility for what was about to happen to the expedition, since he could have foreseen the consequences of a rainy season march, and he could have postponed departure from Gorée until September, or October.

Mungo's journal from mid June onward is largely a record of struggle with the elements, and of sickness and death. The rains, which were often accompanied by high winds and thunderstorms, turned paths into streams, streams into rivers, and rivers in the hill country into raging torrents. Men sick with fever or dysentery struggled to manage recalcitrant asses on difficult paths in the pouring rain. They were harassed by opportunist thieves, who shadowed the caravan, waiting for any opportunity presented by weakness or confusion to dash in and steal whatever they could carry. Food was sometimes short and in the heavy rains it might be impossible to light a fire to cook a meal. When men became too ill to walk, the only way in which they could be carried was by placing them on the backs of horses or asses, with someone in attendance to hold them. When this no longer served, there was no alternative but to leave the sick man behind; if possible in a village, where the chief — for payment — would agree to look after him until he died.

On 4 July the expedition nearly lost Isaaco, who was attacked by a crocodile that seized one of his legs while he was driving asses across a river. Isaaco, with great presence of mind, instantly thrust his fingers into the beast's eyes, the only way of forcing it to release its hold. The crocodile returned to the attack and seized his other leg. Isaaco again drove his fingers into the crocodile's eyes and made his escape. Both Isaaco's legs were badly mauled but after Mungo had treated his wounds and he had been rested for a week, he recovered sufficiently for the caravan to continue its journey.

By 18 July thirteen casualties were recorded, five were dead from fever, dysentery or some other sickness, one had been drowned crossing the Senegal river, four were left behind and three were missing. As the caravan lost strength, with men falling out almost daily, it began to disintegrate and became an easy prey for thieves, who boldly moved in to take whatever they could lay their hands on. Men had only to turn their backs for an instant and a thief would be there to seize a musket or a greatcoat, or drive away an ass. Those who were sick or weak were even stripped of their clothes.

It was not only thieves that preyed upon the expedition, for lions and wild dogs attempted to do so. On one occasion lions stampeded the asses, and Mungo had a close encounter with three lions that he only drove off by advancing toward them and firing his musket. Some of those who were left behind, or who went missing, may well have fallen victim to wild animals.

The expedition finally reached the Niger at Bamako on 19 August, having taken 115 days to cover a distance that Mungo had hoped to cover in less than half that time. The expedition suffered a further nineteen casualties between 18 July and arrival at Bamako, four men having died, six having been left behind, and nine having failed to reach camp after a day's travelling. Of the forty-four Europeans who had left the Gambia, only twelve remained alive and some of them were sick, among them Alexander Anderson. George Scott, the draughtsman, was one of those who died before the expedition reached Bamako.

That the expedition reached the Niger at all, in the face of all the difficulties and all the suffering that had been endured, says much for the courage and discipline of the men. Mungo Park may be criticised for his decision to leave the Gambia in the hot season, just weeks before the start of the rains, and perhaps for a lack of firm leadership in the early days of the march. However, when problems really began in early June, though sick himself for at least part of the time, he was tireless in his efforts to keep the expedition together and to keep it moving forward. He gave what aid he could to the sick, on occasion going back over the day's route to find men who had fallen out through weakness and exhaustion. He carried their loads, placed the men on horses or asses and held them there.

Isaaco and his attendants also deserved credit for getting the expedition through to Bamako. Isaaco was guide and negotiator with chiefs and others, and he helped the expedition in other ways, sending his attendants to look for men and asses that were lost. These attendants also helped with the loads that the sick and weak could not lift or carry, and on one occasion they built a bridge over a swollen stream.

Perhaps not surprisingly, given all the problems of the march, Mungo has relatively little to say in his journal about the economy and society of the countries through which the expedition marched. However, he did make notes on the local method of indigo dyeing in the Gambia. He visited some gold mines near the Falemé river and recorded in detail the mining operation, and the separation process, and at a later stage of the march he observed the process used in the smelting of gold.

The expedition rested for two days in Bamako and then moved down river to the town of Maraboo. Mungo and Alexander Anderson, who were both sick, made the journey in a small canoe, passing through several rapids on the fast flowing Niger, one to two miles wide in this area. Since this canoe was the only one available, Martyn and the remaining men made their way to Maraboo by land. Here Mungo paid Isaaco for his services, with goods to the value of two slaves, with some goodwill additions. He persuaded Isaaco to undertake a mission to Mansong, the king of Segu, by promising to give him all the horses and asses that had survived the journey. Mungo was anxious to secure Mansong's friendship and protection, before the Moors and *slatees* could create problems for him, through whatever influence they might have with the king and his

Mining and washing for gold.

counsellors. Isaaco left for Segu on 28 August, carrying part of the official present.

While waiting for a reply, Mungo decided to treat the persistent dysentery he was suffering from with a heroic dose of calomel, (mercurous chloride, formerly used medicinally as a purgative), that rendered him speechless and sleepless for six days! It also 'cured' his dysentery. He was using what medicines he had, such as calomel and cinchona bark, containing quinine, to treat the men suffering from dysentery or fever, but to no great effect. In the early nineteenth century not enough was known about tropical diseases to devise treatments that would prove effective in more than a handful of cases.

As Mungo waited for news from Isaaco he heard an extremely worrying report, namely that Mansong had killed Isaaco with his own hand, and had sworn to kill all the Europeans who might come to his kingdom. He must have been greatly relieved when one of Mansong's courtiers arrived with a message of welcome from the king, and six canoes in which he was to convey Mungo and his party to the town of Samee, not far from Segu. Six canoes were not sufficient, so the courtier promptly requisitioned one from its owner, giving him a beating into the bargain!

123

At Samee on 19 September, Isaaco returned from his mission. He reported that he had seen Mansong, had delivered Mungo's message, and that the king had agreed to allow the expedition to pass through his country. Isaaco had brought back the presents Mungo had entrusted to him, since Mansong evidently felt it to be more fitting that Mungo should present them to his representative himself. From Isaaco's description of his meeting with Mansong, Mungo reached the conclusion that the king had a superstitious fear of transactions with Europeans, and would not meet them face to face.

Shortly after Isaaco's return, Mungo received a visit from Modibinne, the king's Chief Minister, and several courtiers. Speaking to them in the Mandingo language, Mungo made reference to his previous visit and to Mansong's kindness to him as a destitute stranger. Mungo explained that he intended to follow the Joliba to the sea and hoped thereby to open a route for ships from Britain to bring direct to Segu those quality goods for which Mansong and his people presently paid very high prices to the Moors. Modibinne approved Mungo's plans and assured him of Mansong's protection. Mungo then produced the presents for Mansong — a silver-plated tureen, a pair of double-barrelled guns, pistols, a sabre, several bales of cloth, etc., with more modest presents for Mansong's eldest son, and for Modibinne and the courtiers who had accompanied him. These gifts made a deep impression and Modibinne left for Segu to report to Mansong and deliver the presents. Two days later Modibinne returned with Mansong's response. He offered protection to the expedition throughout his kingdom, and would convey its members to wherever they chose to build their boat. In return for the presents, he undertook to provide Mungo with a good canoe.

Mungo chose Sansanding as the place where he would build his boat and on 26 September the surviving members of the expedition moved there. Three soldiers had died from fever or dysentery during the waiting time at Maraboo and Samee, so there were only nine men left, some of them sick. At Sansanding the expedition lodged with Counti Mamaadi, the elderly *dooty* who had been Mungo's host and protector in 1796. Mungo had to wait until 15 October before Modibinne delivered a canoe, which was found to be half-rotten. While waiting for this canoe to arrive Mungo made an inspection of the town of Sansanding, paying particular attention to the market. In his journal he recorded in detail the goods that were bought and sold there. He also refers to his decision to open a shop selling off surplus goods from the expedition. Mungo needed funds in cowries in case he should have to purchase canoes, but that turned out not to be necessary. Cowries remained useful, since they were a common currency throughout the region, and a good supply would allow the expedition to buy provisions along the river. Mungo's shop did a brisk trade for a few days, but it did not endear him to the local merchants, who appealed to Mansong to seize the expedition's goods and either kill or expel its members. Mansong rejected their appeal, but he was probably anxious for the expedition to leave as soon as possible, before the Moors and *slatees* caused trouble.

A second canoe, in much the same condition as the first one, was eventually obtained and brought down from Segu by Isaaco on 20 October. Since all four carpenters had died, or were lost and presumed dead, responsibility for the construction of a boat fell to Mungo. Working with Private Abraham Bolton, he cut the two canoes in half, discarded the rotten parts and joined the good parts together, following local methods. A deck was then laid down, masts raised, a steering oar fitted, and a shelter constructed at the stern, creating an unusual craft some forty feet in length, six feet wide, flat-bottomed and drawing one foot of water when laden. The sides of the boat were raised to provide protection for those defending the vessel, now named His Majesty's Schooner *Joliba,* against any attackers. Work on the *Joliba* was probably completed around the middle of November.

There were further casualties while the expedition was at Sansanding. Four men died there, among them Alexander Anderson, Mungo's friend and brother-in-law, who finally succumbed to the combined effects of fever and dysentery, on 28 October. The death of his friend and wife's brother affected Mungo deeply, for he recorded in his journal:

> that no event which took place during the journey, ever threw the smallest gloom over my mind, till I laid Mr Anderson in the grave. I then felt myself, as if left a second time lonely and friendless amidst the wilds of Africa.

In the final days at Sansanding, Mungo wrote personal letters to Allison, to Dr Thomas Anderson his father-in-law, to George Scott's father, to Sir Joseph Banks and several others. He also wrote officially to Lord Camden, and sent him the journal recording the proceedings of the expedition. The letters to the bereaved, as always, must have proved hard for Mungo to write, but his words of consolation and appreciation for the life and friendship of the departed, though formal, have the ring of sincerity. In his letter to Lord Camden, Mungo wrote of his determination 'to discover the termination of the Niger or perish in the attempt'. In his letter to Allison, apparently written on the morning of the departure of HMS *Joliba* from Sansanding, Mungo wrote that he did not intend to stop or land anywhere until the expedition reached the coast, and emphasised this decision in the following phrase: 'We this morning have done with all intercourse with the natives'. This was a fateful decision, albeit one that was not adhered to rigorously, but which may have doomed the expedition to destruction.

With the help of Isaaco, Mungo had hired a guide for the next stage of the journey, down the Niger to the Hausa country. The guide, whose name was Amadi Fatouma, came from Khasso, but he was a widely travelled man, who had been to the Gold Coast, Borno and Katsina. He undertook to accompany the expedition down the Niger to Katsina. Since Katsina is not on the Niger, Amadi Fatouma probably meant the small Hausa state of Yauri (Yawuri), that stood on the Niger, and which local traditions suggest was founded by people from Katsina. (Yauri is over 250 miles from Katsina, but is the nearest point on the Niger to that city. The southern part of the Katsina kingdom was only some ninety miles from Yauri.) Mungo also purchased two slaves to assist in the handling of the *Joliba*, since only four members of the expedition now remained alive, in addition to himself — Lieutenant Martyn, Privates Bolton, Connor and Higgins. Private Higgins was a sick man, and probably insane, when the expedition left Sansanding, on or about 20 November 1805.

13

The search for Mungo Park

Mungo Park's final letters do not appear to have reached Britain until about one year after he sent them, but six or seven months before that Sir Joseph Banks had received several reports concerning the expedition and its losses, up to the time of its arrival at Sansanding. In July 1806 the first report of Mungo Park's death was published in *The Times*. Over the next few years *The Times* published several contradictory reports, some claiming that he was dead, others that he was still alive, but a reasonably reliable account of his death was not available in Britain until 1812.

In July 1806, following inquiries made on behalf of the Park and Anderson families, the Secretary of State for War & the Colonies wrote to Major Lloyd at Gorée, instructing him to investigate the matter. Lloyd was unable to find anyone prepared to venture into the interior, but he advised the Secretary of State that reports then current on the Gambia suggested that those members of the expedition who had left Sansanding had all been murdered. This was how matters stood until 1810, after Lloyd's successor at Gorée, Major Charles Maxwell, led a force of 160 soldiers from Gorée in a combined naval and military operation that drove the French from Senegal in July 1809. While Maxwell was in Senegal, he found Isaaco and commissioned him to return to the interior to try and discover what had happened to Mungo Park and his companions. Isaaco returned from the interior in September 1811, having — by great good fortune — encountered Amadi Fatouma, the guide whom Mungo Park had hired for the journey from Sansanding to Katsina. Isaaco recorded his meeting with Amadi Fatouma as follows:

On seeing me, and hearing me mention Mr Park he began to weep; and his first words were, 'They are all dead'. I said 'I am come to see after you, and intend to look every way for you, to know the truth from your own mouth, how they died'. He said that they were lost for ever, and it was useless to make any further inquiry after them;...

Amadi Fatouma gave Isaaco an account of the events that had occurred on the voyage of HMS *Joliba* between Sansanding and Yauri, where he had left the expedition, as previously agreed. Though Amadi Fatouma was not with the expedition when it left Yauri, he had remained in the town, where he was arrested and detained by the king, either because the king felt he had been slighted by the travellers, or because he had not received a present or considered it inadequate. While in custody at Yauri, Amadi Fatouma heard of the death of the remaining European members of the expedition at Bussa, some fifty miles below the river port of Yauri, and on his release he made contact with a slave who had survived the disaster and obtained his account of what had happened. He therefore had an eyewitness account of the death of Mungo Park and his companions. When Isaaco returned to Senegal he was able to provide Lieutenant-Colonel Charles Maxwell, now Governor of Sierra Leone with responsibility for Senegal and Gorée, with an Arabic manuscript account of his own journey, and with his Arabic manuscript transcription of Amadi Fatouma's narrative of Mungo Park's voyage from Sansanding to Bussa. English translations were made of both and these were received in London at the end of January 1812.

Amadi Fatouma's narrative is generally accepted as providing a reasonably reliable, if somewhat incomplete, guide to what happened to the expedition between Sansanding and Yauri. His account of this part of the journey is substantially confirmed by other reports, including those of several North African merchants, or their agents, who were in Timbuktu or Kabara, when HMS *Joliba* approached the latter place; those of Captain Hugh Clapperton, RN, who was in Sokoto in 1824, and at Bussa in 1826; those of Dr Heinrich Barth, who was in the area in 1853–4, and travelled by land along Mungo Park's route for several hundred miles, hearing stories of the passage of the white man's strange canoe along the river, and of the attacks made upon it by the Tuareg, nearly fifty years previously.

Mungo Park does not appear to have made any attempt to secure a letter of introduction from Mansong that he could have used on his way down river and at Timbuktu. He knew from his experiences on the first expedition that a letter of introduction could be of the very greatest importance in securing safe passage from the territory of one ruler to another, and that the lack of such a letter could create difficulties. He also knew that tolls or tribute were normal on passage through the territories of African kings and chiefs. For reasons that are not entirely clear, Mungo appears to have made up his mind that HMS *Joliba* would not halt at the behest of those who felt they had a right to tax travellers, and that force would be used against any who threatened to attack the expedition, or attempted to impede its passage. HMS *Joliba* would be a floating fortress that he would not leave until he reached the termination of the Niger, wherever that might be. The crew were to be prepared for action at all times, each man having fifteen loaded muskets to hand wherewith to repulse any who approached the boat with hostile intent.

There is no doubt but that Mungo had a very great fear of again falling into the hands of the Moors, whom he believed controlled Timbuktu and other places along the river. The political economy of Timbuktu was altogether much more complex than Mungo had been led to believe, and he would not necessarily have received the same kind of treatment from the rulers of that relatively sophisticated and cosmopolitan trading city as he had experienced at the hands of Ali in Ludamar.

From Amadi Fatouma's narrative we learn that on leaving Sansanding, HMS *Joliba* proceeded down river past Silla, where Mungo had turned back in 1796. Here Mungo purchased another slave to assist with the navigation of the boat. Leaving Silla, Mungo took a side channel that connected the Niger with the Bani river, on which lay the important trading city of Djenne, still within the Bambara kingdom of Segu. Here Mansong's protection probably ensured the safe passage of the expedition and Amadi Fatouma records that a bale of cloth was presented to the chief at Djenne. What is not known is whether Mungo obtained any safe-conduct, or letter of introduction, from the chief at Djenne, that might have helped him secure safe passage to Kabara and Timbuktu, though in the light of what was to happen, it seems most unlikely that he did.

Leaving Djenne, the expedition would have passed down the Bani to Mopti, where the Bani joins the Niger, and would have entered the strange country of the inland delta, where the Niger breaks up into several channels that come together again in Lake Debo. Beyond the lake the Niger divides into two main channels and in the rainy season floods a very large area, creating temporary lakes on both banks. These lakes then empty back into the river in the dry season. In this area the expedition clashed with three armed canoes, probably manned by Surka, a sub-group of the Tuareg, who controlled both banks of the Niger for some distance above, and for a considerable distance below Timbuktu. The Surka, if that is who they were, were probably intent on demanding a customary toll, or payment, from the strangers. Mungo was apparently convinced of their hostile intentions and ordered his men to open fire on the canoes, driving them off. Amadi Fatouma's narrative suggests that there may have been two and possibly three more incidents in which hostile canoes were fired on from HMS *Joliba*, in the area between Koriouma and Kabara, the port of Timbuktu. Koriouma is the point at which a side channel leads from the main stream of the Niger to Kabara and it is possible that the Surka attempted to ambush HMS *Joliba*, when she entered the side channel and again when she came back from Kabara. The Surka may then have pursued HMS *Joliba* as she turned into the main stream of the Niger, sailing with the current toward the east. The Surka certainly suffered casualties during these encounters and in one of the reports that Sir Joseph Banks received from a correspondent in Morocco, it was claimed that a Sharif, or a Tuareg Prince, had been killed in one of these exchanges. If this was true, it might explain the repeated attempts to halt the travellers and exact revenge.

Though Amadi Fatouma's narrative has nothing to say about the visit of HMS *Joliba* to Kabara, there is abundant evidence that Mungo took the boat up the side channel to Kabara and remained anchored some distance from the bank for a whole day. A white flag was hoisted on the boat, this no doubt being intended as a signal for a truce and as an invitation for negotiations. However, the signal was not understood and no contact was made. No one from HMS *Joliba* landed at Kabara and no one from the port went out to the boat. Toward evening the anchor was hoisted and HMS *Joliba* returned down the side channel leading to Koriouma and the Niger. Sadly, Mungo Park never did get to see the fabled city of Timbuktu. (The tales told in Europe of the great wealth of Timbuktu related to the long-distant past, and while the city remained a commercial centre of importance, strategically located on important trade routes, it no longer lay at the heart of a great empire, nor had it remained the great centre of Islamic learning it had once been).

Amadi Fatouma's narrative records that one white man died from sickness in the area of Timbuktu, this very probably being Private Higgins. He recalled that the Tuareg made two more attacks on HMS *Joliba* during the descent of the Niger from the area of Timbuktu, one in the area of Bamba, the other to the south of Gao. When Heinrich Barth travelled along this stretch of the Niger, he was told that there were other attacks, particularly in the area between Bamba and Tosaye. However, Amadi Fatouma's account, in what is probably a reference to this area, suggests what may have been a running battle:

> Passed by a village (of which I have forgotten the name), the residence of King Gotoijege; after passing which we encountered sixty canoes coming after us, which we repulsed, and killed a great number of men. Seeing so many killed, and our superiority over them, I took hold of Martyn's hand, saying, 'Martyn, let us cease firing; for we have killed too many already'; on which Martyn wanted to kill me, had not Mr Park interfered...

After Tosaye the Niger turned to the south-east and HMS *Joliba* began to encounter other problems, striking rocks and coming close, on at least two occasions, to being overturned by hippopotami. South of Gao the Niger passes through a stretch of about 100 miles, where there are a series of rapids, some of them dangerous and difficult to navigate. Though Amadi Fatouma mentions only one attack in the area south of Gao, Heinrich Barth encountered people in this area who spoke of two attacks, and he thought there may have been a third, before HMS *Joliba* left the area controlled by the Tuareg. It is not known how many Tuareg were killed in all these attacks, but it is probable there were many casualties. There is no evidence from Amadi Fatouma's narrative that there were any European casualties in the fighting on the Niger, and as he had mentioned the death of one through sickness, it is reasonable to assume that he would have mentioned any other deaths that occurred.

HMS *Joliba* left that part of the Niger river controlled by the Tuareg in the area of the modern city of Niamey, capital of the Republic of Niger. The expedition was now approaching the lands of the Hausa people, which were in turmoil. In February 1804, a revolutionary Islamic movement, under the leadership of the Fulani scholar Shehu Usumanu dan Fodio (Shaikh 'Uthman ibn Fodiye), had challenged the authority of the Hausa king of Gobir, and was in the process of creating a confederation of states that came to be known as the Sokoto Caliphate, after the place where the Shaikh established his headquarters in 1809. At the time Mungo Park's expedition arrived in Yauri, early in 1806, a significant part of what is now north-western Nigeria had fallen to the armies of the *jihad* that the Shehu had declared against infidel and apostate rulers, and those nominally Muslim rulers who combined the practice of Islam with pagan rites and rituals, or who failed to observe and enforce the *shari'a*. However, it would appear that the armies of the *jihad* had not invaded Yauri at the time Mungo Park arrived there, though they probably did do so within a few weeks of his brief visit. In Yauri and neighbouring areas, there was probably considerable uncertainty and apprehension regarding the moves that the Shehu's forces were about to make, and the sudden appearance of the strange vessel on the Niger, here known as the Kwara, may have caused some alarm, and may have been linked in some way with the *jihad*.

Mungo Park and his European companions had not left HMS *Joliba* throughout the entire voyage, though from time to time they had set Amadi Fatouma ashore to buy provisions. At Yauri, where Amadi Fatouma would leave the expedition, Mungo remained on board the boat while Amadi distributed gifts to the chief and some others at the place where the boat had anchored, the king's residence being a few miles inland. The chief, probably acting on the king's instructions, responded with a good supply of provisions, and Amadi purchased more. Mungo had given Amadi Fatouma what appear to have been some rather paltry items as a present for the king, but Amadi apparently left them with the chief to give to the king, who may not have received them.

The king certainly knew of Mungo's presence, and is reported to have come down to the riverside to meet him. The king is said to have sent messages to Mungo recommending that he continue his journey by land, or if that was not possible that he take a guide supplied by the king. Mungo remained on board the boat and either declined to meet the king, or left before a meeting could be arranged. To have left Yauri without greeting the king was an insulting thing to have done, and Mungo would have known this. It suggests that he no longer cared about such things, and that all that mattered to him now was getting down the river to the sea in the shortest possible time. If he was continuing to make astronomical observations, as he had done on the march from the Gambia to Sansanding, he would have realised that the Niger was flowing towards the Atlantic ocean in the area of the Bights of Benin and Biafra.

HMS *Joliba* left the port of Yauri without a guide, pilot or interpreter, heading south with the flow of the current. Some fifty miles below Yauri the river narrows and passes through a series of rapids, some of them very dangerous. HMS *Joliba* struck the rocks in rapids opposite the town of Bussa and lodged there. What happened immediately before and after she struck the rocks is and will remain something of a mystery, but there are two main theories, with a number of variations and qualifications.

The first theory is that the boat was attacked by the people of Bussa, then struck the rocks and became lodged there. Those on board the boat used their muskets in self-defence and killed or wounded many people. Mungo and his companions eventually ran out of ammunition and rather than be taken alive jumped overboard and were drowned. A variant explanation is that the boat struck the rocks and its occupants were attacked by the Bussa people as they struggled to free it.

The second theory is that the Bussa people tried to warn those in the boat that they were approaching dangerous rapids but their shouts and gestures were misunderstood. With no guide or interpreter, those on the boat were unable to communicate with those on shore, and following the practice they had adopted in the Tuareg country, they fired on those they assumed were hostile. Shocked and outraged, the Bussa people responded to what they saw as an unprovoked attack and a general *mêlée* followed. At some point the boat struck the rocks and lodged there, the events concluding with Mungo and his companions leaping from the boat and drowning. There is general agreement that one, or possibly two, of the slaves in the boat survived the attack, though badly wounded.

Mention must be made of an explanation that has been offered for the attack by the Bussa people, if that is what actually occurred. The people of Bussa are said to have believed that those in the boat were spies, or some sort of advance party for the army of the *jihad,* and for that reason they were attacked. This is not implausible, and later in 1806 a *jihad* army did enter and waste parts of Borgu. However, Bussa and the other states of Borgu were not conquered or brought within the Sokoto Caliphate during the nineteenth century.

Amadi Fatouma's account, based on the information he had received from a slave who survived the disaster at Bussa, differs little from the first theory except that it places responsibility for the attack on Yauri. The slave told Amadi that the king of Yauri was offended by Mungo's behaviour and sent a force to stop him at Bussa. This is possible and there is one other account that confirms it, though adding that the king's instructions were that the expedition should be halted and its members brought back to Yauri, but not harmed and certainly not killed. Amadi was also told by the surviving slave that there were four white men in the boat at the time of the attack and that Mungo Park and John Martyn jumped into the river holding the two privates, who presumably could not swim.

Other accounts of what happened at Bussa, some of them impossible or wildly improbable, have been put forward. They were based on scraps of information collected at many places over a long period of time. The most damaging were those that suggested that Mungo Park and his companions were held captive somewhere in the interior, since these gave encouragement to his family's belief that he was still alive. On the basis of some of these wild tales, Thomas Park, Mungo's second son, travelled to West Africa in search of his father. Thomas Park died in the interior of the Gold Coast in October 1827.

Mungo Park, John Martyn and the two soldiers — probably Privates Abraham Bolton and John Connor, died from drowning near Bussa on the Niger, most probably in January or February 1806. The body of one of them, though it is not known whom, was reported to have been recovered from the river and to have been buried on the island of Kainji, downstream from Bussa. Today Kainji island is the site of a massive dam across the Niger. The town of Bussa, and the place where Mungo Park and his companions died, today lie deep below the waters of the Kainji Lake.

14

Mungo Park: tragedy and achievement

Mungo Park did not solve the mystery of the Niger, though he must have believed that he was well on the way to doing so, when he sailed from Yauri. When Amadi Fatouma's narrative was received in Britain it told the geographers very little, since it contained no indication of distances or of the changes in the direction of flow of the Niger, and in particular it said nothing of the Niger's turn to the south-east after passing Timbuktu. Partial answers to the geographic questions came from Hugh Clapperton's expedition to Sokoto in 1824, when Mohammed Bello, Caliph of Sokoto, told him what he knew of the course of the Niger, and explained the geography of the Hausa states and their neighbours, relative to one another. Hugh Clapperton saw the Niger and confirmed an important part of what Caliph Bello had told him, when he visited Bussa on his way to Sokoto from Badagry on the Atlantic coast in 1826. Final resolution of the riddle of the Niger did not come until 1830, when the brothers Richard and John Lander travelled down the Niger from Bussa to the sea.

Mungo Park's achievement lies not so much in geography as in the account he gave of Africa and Africans in *Travels in the Interior Districts of Africa*. Mungo had empathy and understanding, recognising in the Africans he met the human qualities that all men share. In short he was no racist. He was most definitely not one of those who maintained that the African was an inferior being, a widely held though not unchallenged view in Europe and the Americas in the eighteenth century, that gained strength from pseudo-scientific theorising in the nineteenth century, and remains with us at the beginning of the twenty-first century as a poisonous legacy.

Mungo's empathy with the Africans he met on the first expedition may owe more than a little to his origins in what was in many respects a traditional agrarian society, with a relatively simple technology, just one step removed from subsistence farming. The values of that society were essentially peasant values, rooted in the land and in close family relationships. On his first expedition Mungo's interaction with Africans was generally cordial and when it was not, as in Ludamar and other places where he encountered intolerant Moors, he made the effort to understand the reasons for their antipathy towards him. In Africa, as in Scotland or anywhere in Europe, people could be kind or cruel, generous or mean, hospitable or hostile, liberal in spirit or deeply prejudiced, honest or deceitful. Mungo was well aware that Africa had a political and economic environment that was much like that in Europe, a place where competing individuals, interests and factions might struggle for power and wealth. There were monarchies with constitutions founded in custom, and with developed systems of law and administration. Wars in Africa were generally fought for much the same reasons as in Europe — ambition to enlarge the territory of the state and the desire to posses the resources of others, refusal to submit to tyrannical or alien rule, a conviction that it was right to impose a religion, etc.

Early in Mungo Park's residence in Africa he learnt some golden rules — be respectful towards the people and their laws, customs and institutions. Learn the language, eat the food that the people eat and as far as possible conform to local norms of behaviour. It was of the utmost importance to respect the dignity of an African ruler, listen to him and whenever possible take his advice. It was always desirable, often essential, to obtain a safe conduct or a letter of introduction from the ruler, when travelling from one kingdom or chiefdom to another. It was advisable to be patient and to be prepared to negotiate the terms of travel through a country.

The tragedy of Mungo Park is that by the time he made his second expedition into Africa he seems either to have forgotten or to have ignored much of what he had learnt on his first expedition. It was not entirely his fault that the second expedition was such a disaster, but he did make mistakes that have tarnished his reputation. Responsibility for the fatal timing of the second expedition rests heavily with Sir Joseph Banks and Lord Camden, but Mungo could have refused the commission on the grounds of inordinate delay and consequent hazard, and demanded that it be rescheduled to the next dry season. Mungo had achieved a certain fame, and he knew Africa in a way that Banks and Camden did not. Mungo's fame and his knowledge of Africa should have given him the authority to speak frankly and to be heard, and he might well have had the significant support of Major Rennell, had he done so. Regrettably, Mungo abdicated the responsibility that goes with fame and knowledge when he accepted the commission to take an expedition into the interior of Africa on the eve of the rainy season. Once that decision had been taken and the expedition had left Gorée, there was virtually no chance of it reaching the Niger without suffering very severe losses, and he must have known this, yet he still went ahead.

It can be argued that Mungo allowed himself to become an 'Instrument in the hands of a good Director', to use the words Banks had applied to Mungo during their disagreements over the mission to Australia in 1798. Did Mungo see himself as an 'Instrument' subject to the direction of Sir Joseph Banks, the British Government and the Crown? The answer is that at one level he probably did, but there are reasons for thinking that Mungo also thought of himself as an 'Instrument' in the hands of that Providence that had seen him through the horrors of Ludamar, and much else besides, during the first expedition. While Mungo may have retained his ambition to achieve fame and distinction, this is of rather less importance in explaining his conduct on the second expedition, than his conviction that he was in some sense a chosen man, one whose destiny it was to solve an ancient question. He had failed to solve it in 1796, yet Providence had protected him, and now gave him another opportunity. He had hoped and prayed for this opportunity while riding the Peebleshire hills in winter, or working for the relief of the sick and needy in that 'miserable den' of a surgery in Peebles. How could he not seize this new opportunity?

Mungo's rational mind should have told him that an expedition into the West African interior during the rainy season was a doomed enterprise, but his reason in this matter was no longer wholly engaged, for he now saw himself as a Chosen Man. Why else this second opportunity and the chance to redeem what he had come to regard as his failure on the first expedition? Providence had protected him then, how could it not do so now? It was in this state of mind that Mungo Park approached the second expedition, with disastrous consequences. As a Chosen Man, Mungo may also have believed that he was a Justified Man, that is to say one whose actions were justified by the ends they served. Nothing seems to have shaken Mungo's belief in himself as a Chosen Man, appointed to complete a Mission under the direction of Providence, until the death of Alexander Anderson, and by then it was impossible to turn back, or undo what had been done. When reason returned Mungo could only contemplate responsibility for the deaths of thirty-seven men, and the prospect of a hazardous voyage into the unknown. Perhaps weighed down by guilt and with his capacity for rational thought and judgement seriously compromised, he does not appear to have taken any steps to ensure safe and unimpeded passage through the territories controlled by the Tuareg.

Mungo took the decision to voyage down the Niger without paying tribute or customs to those who believed they had a right to it, and without any letter of introduction or safe-conduct. Inevitably his descent of the Niger in HMS *Joliba* became a running battle with the Tuareg, determined to insist on their rights and enraged by his high-handed behaviour. The scale of Tuareg casualties is not known, but was severe enough for Mungo Park to be remembered with bitterness and anger by the Tuareg for many years to come. Mungo fatally compounded this error by refusing to meet with the king of Yauri, who could and probably would have provided him with a safe-conduct, and a guide and interpreter for a considerable distance down the river, if he had been treated with courtesy and respect. The Mungo Park of the second expedition was not the man who had made that epic journey between 1795 and 1797. Mungo Park's second expedition deserves to be remembered as an ill-conceived and bloody enterprise, grimly foreshadowing some other European expeditions to the African interior in the latter part of the nineteenth century.

Mungo Park remains of interest to us today primarily for the account he gave of Africa and Africans within the pages of his *Travels in the Interior Districts of Africa*. While this book is certainly a tale of courage in the face of adversity, it is a great deal more than that. Within its pages we are introduced to Africa as it was, and as it remains, to some degree. We find within the book so many interesting and instructive characters, from Ali of Ludamar to Karfa Taura at Kamaila; and the many nameless people, especially women, who treated a stranger with kindness and goodwill. Our ancestors learnt from Mungo Park, and some other early travellers in the African continent, that Africans are much like Europeans, human beings with the same needs, the same capacity for good and evil. This is a lesson that needs constantly to be renewed in the face of ignorance and blind prejudice. Mungo Park's narrative of his first expedition to Africa still has things to say to us all two centuries after its first publication.

INDEX

PLACES TO VISIT

Foulshiels: Mungo Park's birthplace. The shell of the Park family home has been preserved thanks to the efforts of the Saltire Society, other organisations and individuals. It stands on the right hand side of the A708 Selkirk to Moffat road, some four miles from Selkirk. (There is no assigned parking space for visitors to Foulshiels, and great care should be taken when parking on the A708 in the area of the cottage.)

Selkirk: Sir Walter Scott's Courthouse Museum. This building, formerly Selkirk's Town House and Sheriff Courthouse, dominates the Market Square at Selkirk. Today it houses a Museum featuring the life and work of Sir Walter Scott, and the lives and works of his friends James Hogg 'the Ettrick Shepherd', and Mungo Park. A wall display features Mungo Park's travels in Africa, and a display cabinet contains a few of his personal belongings, including a Royal Africa Corps jacket, a sword, walking stick, pocket watch, etc. The cabinet also holds a boxed book of Hymns and Psalms that belonged to Alexander Anderson, Mungo Park's friend and companion on the second expedition. This was recovered at Bussa by the Lander brothers in 1830, and restored to the Anderson

family on the insistence of James Hogg. [Only one other item from Mungo Park's second expedition was ever recovered and brought back to Britain, a book of astronomical tables that belonged to Mungo Park. This was purchased by Lt John Glover RN, at a Nupe town, down river from Bussa, in 1858. It is now in the possession of the Royal Geographic Society in London].

Selkirk: The Mungo Park Memorial Statue. The statue stands at the north-east end of the High Street in Selkirk, facing what was the Anderson family home. The statue of Mungo Park by Andrew Currie of Darnick was erected in 1859. The four statues of African figures at the base of the column were added in 1906, and the two bronze panels in 1912. The statues and panels are the work of Thomas Clapperton of Galashiels.

Edinburgh: The Museum of Scotland has on display a brass door plate from the house occupied by Mungo Park when he was a surgeon in Peebles, from October 1801 to May 1804.

Peebles: Mungo Park's residence in Peebles is commemorated by a plaque on a house in the Northgate, and by a plaque marking the site of his surgery on the High Street.

SELECT BIBLIOGRAPHY

The Works of Mungo Park

Travels in the Interior Districts of Africa, Performed in the Years 1795, 1796 and 1797 by Mungo Park, with Geographical Illustration of Africa by Major Rennell, London, 1799.

The Journal of a Mission in the Interior of Africa in the Year 1805 by Mungo Park, with an Account of the Life of Mr Park (by John Wishaw) (including Isaaco's and Amadi Fatouma's Journals and, in the second edition, some additional material with the Account of the Life). London, 1815.

"Descriptions of Eight New Fishes from Sumatra" by Mungo Park, ALS. *Transactions of the Linnean Society*, Vol. 3, (1797), 33–9.

Two poems by Mungo Park are known to have been printed; "Sleep on my Sweet Babie" is reproduced in this work; the "Song for the Tweeddale Cavalry" may be found in *The Life of Mungo Park*, by H B.

Biographies

The Life of Mungo Park by H B, Edinburgh, 1835.

The Life and Travels of Mungo Park anon, Chambers, Edinburgh, 1838.

Mungo Park and the Niger by Joseph Thomson, London, 1890.

Niger: The Life of Mungo Park by Lewis Grassic Gibbon, Edinburgh, 1934.

Mungo Park and the Quest for the Niger by Stephen Gwynn, Bristol, 1934.

Mungo Park the African Traveler, by Kenneth Lupton, Oxford, 1979.

"African Exploration and Human Understanding" by E A Ayandele in his *African Historical Studies*, 1979. [A lecture for the Mungo Park bicentenary commemorations at the University of Edinburgh, 2 December, 1971, published by Edinburgh University Press, 1972.]

Scotland

Buchan, James W & Paton, H (Rev) *A History of Peebleshire*, Glasgow, 1925–7.

Craig Brown, T *History of Selkirkshire, or Chronicles of Ettrick Forest*, Edinburgh, 1886.

Daiches, David, Jones, P & J (Eds) *A Hotbed of Genius. The Scottish Enlightenment, 1730– 1790*, Edinburgh, 1986.

Rosner, Lisa *Medical Education in the Age of Improvement; Edinburgh Students and Apprentices, 1760–1826*, Edinburgh, 1991.

Smout, T C *A History of the Scottish People, 1560–1830*, Glasgow, 1985.

Youngson, A J *The Making of Classical Edinburgh*, Edinburgh, 1966.

Geography of Africa & the African Association

Africanus, Leo *History & Description of Africa*, London, 1896.

Bovill, E W *The Golden Trade of the Moors*, London, 2nd edition, 1968.

Hallett, R *The Penetration of Africa to 1815*, London, 1965.

Hallett, R *Records of the African Association, 1788–1831*, London, 1964.

West Africa: The Historical Setting

Ajayi, J F A & Crowder, M *History of West Africa*, London, 1971 & 1974 (2 vols).

Last, M *The Sokoto Caliphate*, London, 1967.

Trimingham, J S *Islam in West Africa*, Oxford, 1959.

The Slave Trade & Slavery in West Africa

Blackburn, R *The Overthrow of Colonial Slavery, 1776–1848*, London, 1990.

Lovejoy, P *Transformations in Slavery: A History of Slavery in Africa*, Cambridge, 1983.

Rawley, J A *The Transatlantic Slave Trade: A History*, NY/ London, 1981.

The search for Mungo Park and the later exploration of the Niger

Barth, H *Travels and Discoveries in North and Central Africa: Being a Journal of an Expedition undertaken under the auspices of H.B.M.'s Government in the Years 1849–55*. London, 1965 (Reprint of the 1857 edition).

Bovill, E W (Ed) *Missions to the Niger*, Cambridge, 1964–66. 4 vols. Vol 1 contains the journal of Friedrich Hornemann (1797–8) and the letters of Major Alexander Gordon Laing (1824–6). [Hornemann is referred to in the text. In 1826, Major Laing became the first European in modern times to visit Timbuktu. Laing was bitterly critical of Mungo Park's behaviour towards the Tuareg during his voyage down the Niger in 1805–6]. Vols 2–4 contain much material relating to the Bornu Mission of 1822–5, including the narratives of Major Dixon Denham and Captain Hugh Clapperton, RN. Captain Clapperton's narrative of his journey to Sokoto in Vol 4 contains a record of his meetings with Sultan Mohammed Bello, who told him what he knew about Mungo Park's voyage and death.

Clapperton, Hugh (Capt) *Journal of a Second Expedition into the Interior of Africa from the Bight of Benin to Soccatoo; to which is added the Journal of Richard Lander from Kano to the sea-coast, partly by a more easterly route*. London, 1966 (Reprint of 1829 edition).

Lander, Richard & John *Journal of an Expedition to explore the course and termination of the Niger; with a narrative of a voyage down that river to its termination*. London, 1832.